JUMP-START *your* QUILTING™

Edited by Jeanne Stauffer

HOUSE of
WHITE
BIRCHES

PUBLISHERS
SINCE 1947

Jump-Start Your Quilting™

Editor **Jeanne Stauffer**
Art Director **Brad Snow**
Publishing Services Director **Brenda Gallmeyer**

Editorial Assistant **Stephanie Smith**
Assistant Art Director **Nick Pierce**
Copy Supervisor **Deborah Morgan**
Copy Editors **Mary O'Donnell, Amanda Scheerer**
Technical Editor **Sandra L. Hatch**
Technical Proofreader **Angie Buckles**

Production Artist Supervisor **Erin Augsburger**
Graphic Artists **Glenda Chamberlain, Edith Teegarden**
Production Assistants **Marj Morgan, Judy Neuenschwander**
Technical Artist **Connie Rand**

Photography Supervisor **Tammy Christian**
Photography **Andrew Johnston, Matthew Owen**
Photo Stylists **Tammy Liechty, Tammy Steiner**

Jump-Start Your Quilting is published by DRG, 306 East Parr Road, Berne, IN 46711.
Copyright © 2011 DRG. All rights reserved. This publication may not be reproduced
in part or in whole without written permission from the publisher.

Printed in China
Library of Congress Control Number: 2010926440
Hardcover ISBN: 978-1-59217-314-3
Softcover ISBN: 978-1-59217-315-0

RETAIL STORES: If you would like to carry this book or any other DRG publications,
visit DRGwholesale.com.

Every effort has been made to ensure that the instructions in this publication
are complete and accurate. We cannot, however, take responsibility for human
error, typographical mistakes or variations in individual work. Please visit
ClotildeCustomerCare.com to check for pattern updates.

DRGbooks.com

1 2 3 4 5 6 7 8 9 10

Welcome

Quilters today say that the biggest problem they have is finding the time to quilt. Yes, it does take a certain amount of time to stitch a quilt, but we've found a way to help you with your time crunch. If you use precut fabric packs to make a quilt or quilted project, you will save part of the time you usually spend cutting fabric, and you will save part of the time you usually spend selecting fabric since the packs usually feature one coordinated fabric line.

Of course, with the time saved you will want to make even more quilts, and we have a book full of projects for you to make. If you love classic quilts, there are instructions for making seven traditional quilt designs that are quicker than ever with precuts. If you want to use your time to make gifts for family, friends and even the dog, you'll find eight easy-with-precut-fabric gift designs.

Pull out all the stops and enjoy those special occasions of the year even more with designs stitched quickly from precut fabrics. You'll be able to complete your projects on time, so you can start celebrating early. If you want to stitch a few projects to decorate your own home, there are instructions for 12 household items that will make your home look better than ever.

If you only like to make quilts, you can now make more of them in the same amount of time if you use precut fabric packs. These designs may be easy, and you can stitch them together quickly, but notice also how beautiful they are. These are quilt patterns that you will want to make over and over.

There's no time to waste. Buy those fabric packs and start quilting now.

Jeanne Stauffer

Contents

Practical Precuts

Fast Favorite Quilts

Classic Quilts With Precuts

Take the next step with precut fabrics. Use them to create traditional quilt designs. In this chapter, you'll find seven designs—a one-block Log Cabin quilt, Dream Windows nap quilt, Hunter's Star variation table topper, friendship wall quilt, Ohio Star throw, Cake Stand bed runner and a Wild Goose Chase throw. All are examples of traditional quilt designs that are quicker than ever with precuts.

Sparkling Stars

This variation of the traditional Hunter's Star block is much easier when you use 2½" strips and 5" squares.

DESIGN BY CONNIE RAND

PROJECT NOTES

The package of 2½" precut strips should include lights and darks, and two contrasting colors for the A and B star points. Red and blue prints were used in the sample.

PROJECT SPECIFICATIONS

Skill Level: Intermediate
Quilt Size: 48" x 48"
Block Size: 12" x 12"
Number of Blocks: 16

MATERIALS

- 10 each red and blue 2½" by fabric width strips (A/B)
- 6 each light and dark 2½" by fabric width strips (E/F)
- 5 dark 2½" by fabric width strips for binding
- 32 light 5" x 5" squares
- 32 dark 5" x 5" squares
- Batting 56" x 56"
- Backing 56" x 56"
- Neutral-color all-purpose thread
- Basic sewing tools and supplies

Cutting

1. Prepare templates using patterns given; cut pieces from the 2½"-wide strips as shown in Figure 1 and following instructions given on E/F and A/B templates. ***Note:*** *Strips are wider than template pieces. Piece A/B is not the same size on all sides, so be sure to mark one side and add the mark on the seam as shown on pattern for matching to piece E/F.*

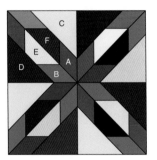

Hunter's Star Variation
12" x 12" Block
Make 16

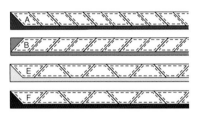

Figure 1

2. Trim each 5" x 5" light and dark square to 4⅞" x 4⅞"; cut each square in half on one diagonal to make 64 each light C and dark D triangles.

Completing the Blocks

1. Sew B to F to A and add C to make a light unit as shown in Figure 2; press seams toward F and C. Repeat to make 64 light units.

Figure 2

Figure 3

2. Sew B to E to A and add D to make a dark unit as shown in Figure 3; press seams toward E and D. Repeat to make 64 dark units.

Sparkling Stars
Placement Diagram 48" x 48"

3. Join one each light and dark unit to make a block quarter as shown in Figure 4; press seam toward the light unit. Repeat to make 64 block quarters.

Figure 4   Figure 5

4. Join four block quarters to complete one Hunter's Star Variation block as shown in Figure 5; press seams in directions shown by arrows, again referring to Figure 5.

5. Repeat step 4 to complete 16 Hunter's Star Variation blocks.

Completing the Top

1. Join four blocks to make a row; press seams in one direction. Repeat to make four rows.

2. Join the rows to complete the pieced top, alternating pressing direction of rows when joining; press seams in one direction.

Finishing the Quilt

1. Refer to Finishing Your Quilt on page 176 to sandwich, quilt and bind your quilt to finish. ***Note:*** *The quilt shown was quilted through the red and blue diamonds with matching thread and a fancy machine stitch, and ¼" inside the C/D triangles using light thread in the light C pieces and dark thread in the dark D pieces.* ◼

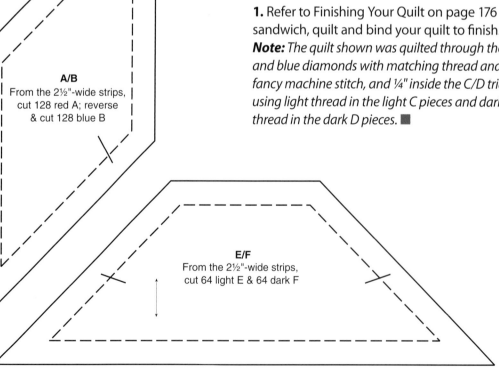

A/B
From the 2½"-wide strips, cut 128 red A; reverse & cut 128 blue B

E/F
From the 2½"-wide strips, cut 64 light E & 64 dark F

Quick Cake Stand Runner

Piece the top of this runner in a weekend using 10" precut fabric squares and Thangles for the triangles.

DESIGN BY JULIA DUNN

PROJECT SPECIFICATIONS

Skill Level: Beginner
Runner Size: 88¾" x 18¼"
Block Size: 10" x 10"
Number of Blocks: 6

MATERIALS

- 6 sets of 2 coordinating 10" x 10" squares—one light, one dark in each set
- ½ yard cream mottled
- 1 yard gold tonal
- 1 yard burgundy print
- Batting 97" x 27"
- Backing 97" x 27"
- Neutral-color all-purpose thread
- Quilting thread
- Thangles for 2" finished half-square triangle units
- Basic sewing tools and supplies

Cutting

1. Select one set of 10" x 10" dark and light squares. Cut one 2½" x 10" strip for A and B as shown in Figure 1.

Figure 1

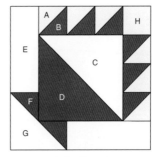

Cake Stand
10" x 10" Block
Make 6

2. From the remainder of the light square, cut one 2½" x 2½" H square as shown in Figure 2.

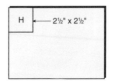

Figure 2

3. From the remainder of the dark square, cut one 2⅞" x 2⅞" square and one 6⅞" x 6⅞" square as shown in Figure 3. Cut the 6⅞" x 6⅞" square in half on one diagonal to make two D triangles. Discard one D triangle. Cut the 2⅞" x 2⅞" square in half on one diagonal to make two F triangles.

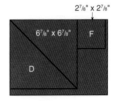

Figure 3

4. Repeat steps 1–3 with each set of squares.

5. Cut two 2½" by fabric width strips cream mottled; subcut strips into (12) 6½" E rectangles.

6. Cut one 6⅞" by fabric width strip cream mottled; subcut strip into three 6⅞" (C) squares and three 4⅞" x 4⅞" (G) squares. Cut each square in half on one diagonal to make six each C and G triangles.

7. Cut two 15⅜" by fabric width strips gold tonal; subcut strips into three 15⅜" squares and two 8" x 8" squares. Cut each 15⅜" square on both diagonals to make 12 J triangles. Discard two triangles. Cut each 8" square in half on one diagonal to make four I triangles.

8. Cut five 2½" by fabric width strips burgundy print. Join strips on short ends to make one long strip; press seams open. Subcut strip into two 85¼" K strips.

9. Cut one 2½" by fabric width strip burgundy print; subcut strip into two 18¾" L strips.

10. Cut six 2¼" by fabric width strips burgundy print for binding.

Completing the Blocks

1. Using one light A strip and one dark B strip, follow directions with the Thangles product to make six A-B half-square triangle units for each block.

2. To complete one Cake Stand block, sew a C triangle to a D triangle along the diagonal; press seam toward D.

3. Join three A-B units to make an A-B strip as shown in Figure 4; press seams in one direction. Repeat to make a reverse A-B strip.

Figure 4

4. Sew an A-B strip to one side of the C-D unit as shown in Figure 5; press seam toward the A-B strip.

Figure 5

5. Sew an H square to the B end of the reversed A-B strip and add to the pieced unit as shown in Figure 6; press seam away from H and toward the pieced strip.

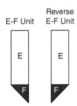

Figure 6

6. Sew F to E to complete an E-F unit referring to Figure 7; press seam toward E. Repeat to make a reverse E-F unit, again referring to Figure 7.

Figure 7

7. Sew the E-F and reverse E-F units to the D sides of the pieced unit as shown in Figure 8; press seams toward E-F and reverse E-F units.

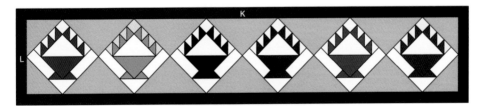

Figure 8

Quick Cake Stand Runner
Placement Diagram 88¾" x 18¼"

8. Sew a G triangle to the F ends of the pieced unit to complete one Cake Stand block referring to Figure 9; press seams toward G.

Figure 9

9. Repeat steps 2–8 with each of the remaining five sets of pieces to complete a total of six Cake Stand blocks.

Completing the Runner Top

1. Arrange and join the Cake Stand blocks with the I and J triangles in diagonal rows as shown in Figure 10; press seams toward I and J triangles.

Figure 10

2. Join the diagonal rows to complete the pieced center; press seams in one direction.

3. Sew a K strip to opposite long sides and the L strips to the short ends of the pieced center to complete the runner top; press seams toward K and L strips.

Finishing the Runner

1. Refer to Finishing Your Quilt on page 176 to sandwich, quilt and bind your runner to finish. ■

Piecing A-B units without Thangles

Instead of cutting the 2½" x 10" strips from each 10" x 10" square, cut three 2⅞" x 2⅞" light and dark squares from each set. Cut each square in half on one diagonal to make six light A and six dark B triangles from each set. Keeping fabrics in sets, sew an A triangle to a B triangle along the diagonal; press seam toward B. Trim dog-ears. Repeat to make six A-B units for one block.

21

21" x 18"

Wild Goose Chase in Red

There is something special about a two-color quilt. Use fat quarters to jump-start this traditional quilt design in red and white.

DESIGN BY AVIS SHIRER
QUILTED BY SUE URICH

PROJECT SPECIFICATIONS

Skill Level: Intermediate
Quilt Size: 45¼" x 56¾"
Block Size: 9¼" x 9¼"
Number of Blocks: 12

MATERIALS

- 1 fat quarter deep red solid for block centers and sashing squares
- 4 red print fat quarters for block side and corner triangles
- 8 assorted red fat quarters for Flying Geese units
- 8 assorted light-color fat quarters for Flying Geese backgrounds
- ½ yard cream mottled for sashing
- ⅝ yard burgundy stripe for inner border
- ⅝ yard burgundy-with-cream polka dots for binding
- ¾ yard burgundy print for outer border
- Batting 53" x 65"
- Backing 53" x 65"
- Neutral-color all-purpose thread
- Quilting thread
- Basic sewing tools and supplies

Cutting

1. Cut two 2⅝" x 21" strips deep red solid; subcut strips into (12) 2⅝" E squares.

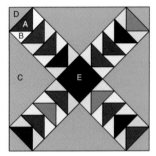

Wild Goose Chase
9¼" x 9¼" Block
Make 12

2. Cut one 2¾" x 21" strip deep red solid; subcut strip into six 2¾" G squares.

3. Cut a total of (32) 1⅝" x 21" strips light-color fat quarters; subcut strips into a total of (384) 1⅝" B squares.

4. Cut a total of (16) 2⅝" x 21" strips assorted red fat quarters; subcut strips into a total of (192) 1⅝" A rectangles.

5. Cut a total of (12) 7⅜" x 7⅜" squares from the four red print fat quarters; cut each square on both diagonals to make 12 sets of four matching C triangles.

6. Cut a total of three sets of two 2⅜" x 2⅜" squares from each red print fat quarter; cut each square in half on one diagonal to make a total of 48 D triangles (12 matching sets of four). Pin a matching set of four D triangles to each matching set of four C triangles.

Wild Goose Chase in Red
Placement Diagram 45¼" x 56¾"

3. Trim seam to ¼" and press B to the right side, again referring to Figure 1.

4. Repeat with a second matching B on the opposite end of A to complete one Flying Geese unit as shown in Figure 2.

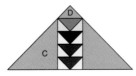

Figure 2

5. Repeat steps 2–4 to complete 192 Flying Geese units.

6. To complete one block, select one E square, 16 Flying Geese units and one set each matching C and D triangles.

7. Join four Flying Geese units to make a pieced strip as shown in Figure 3; press seams in one direction. Repeat to make four pieced strips.

Figure 3

7. Cut five 2¾" by fabric width strips cream mottled; subcut strips into (17) 9¾" F strips.

8. Cut two 3¼" x 38¼" I strips burgundy stripe.

9. Cut two 3¼" x 41¾" H strips burgundy stripe.

10. Cut five 4¼" by fabric width strips burgundy print. Join strips on short ends to make one long strip; press seams open. Subcut strip into two 49¾" J strips and two 45¾" K strips.

11. Cut six 2½" by fabric width strips burgundy-with-cream polka dots for binding.

Completing the Blocks

1. Draw a diagonal line from corner to corner on each B square.

2. Select two matching B squares. Place a B square right sides together on one end of an A rectangle and stitch on the marked line as shown in Figure 1.

Figure 1

8. Sew a C triangle to opposite sides of a pieced strip and add D to make a corner unit as shown in Figure 4; press seams toward C and D triangles. Repeat to make two corner units.

Figure 4

9. Join two pieced strips with E and add D to each end to make the center strip as shown in Figure 5; press seams toward E and D.

Figure 5

10. Sew a corner unit to opposite sides of the center strip to complete one Wild Goose Chase block referring to Figure 6; press seams away from the center strip.

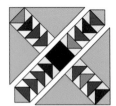

Figure 6

11. Repeat steps 6–10 to complete a total of 12 Wild Goose Chase blocks.

Completing the Quilt Top

1. Join three Wild Goose Chase blocks with two F strips to make a block row as shown in Figure 7; press seams toward F strips. Repeat to make four block rows.

Figure 7

2. Join two G squares and three F strips to make a sashing strip as shown in Figure 8; press seams toward F strips. Repeat to make three sashing strips.

Figure 8

3. Join the block rows with the sashing strips, beginning and ending with a block row; press seams toward sashing rows.

4. Sew an H strip to opposite long sides and I strips to the top and bottom of the pieced center; press seams toward H and I strips.

5. Sew a J strip to opposite long sides and K strips to the top and bottom of the pieced center; press seams toward J and K strips to complete the quilt top.

Finishing the Quilt

1. Refer to Finishing Your Quilt on page 176 to sandwich, quilt and bind your quilt to finish. ■

75
5" x 5"

1
21" x 18"

Charming Ohio Star Throw

Using 5" charm packs and an easy method to create quarter-square triangles makes this classic quilt quick and easy to stitch.

DESIGN BY JULIA DUNN

PROJECT SPECIFICATIONS

Skill Level: Beginner
Throw Size: 54" x 54"
Block Size: 9" x 9"
Number of Blocks: 25

MATERIALS

- 25 sets of 2 matching 5" x 5" charm squares (A)
- 25 (5" x 5") coordinating marbled squares
- 1 fat quarter dark green mottled
- ⅔ yard dark brown mottled
- 2⅞ yards cream mottled
- Batting 62" x 62"
- Backing 62" x 62"
- Neutral-color all-purpose thread
- Quilting thread
- Basic sewing tools and supplies

Cutting

1. Cut seven 5" by fabric width strips cream mottled; subcut strips into (50) 5" B squares.

2. Cut nine 3½" by fabric width strips cream mottled; subcut strips into (100) 3½" C squares.

3. Cut three 9½" by fabric width strips cream mottled; subcut strips into (60) 2" E strips.

4. Cut two 2" x 21" strips dark green mottled; subcut strips into (16) 2" F squares.

5. Cut one 2" by fabric width strip dark brown mottled; subcut strip into (20) 2" G squares.

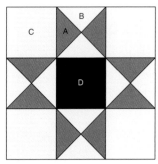

Ohio Star
9" x 9" Block
Make 25

6. Cut six 2¼" by fabric width strips dark brown mottled for binding.

7. Cut (25) 3½" x 3½" D squares from the 5" x 5" marbled squares.

Completing the Blocks

1. To complete one Ohio Star block, select two matching 5" x 5" A squares, two B squares, one coordinating D square and four C squares.

2. Draw a diagonal line from corner to corner on the wrong side of each B square.

3. Place a B square right sides together with an A square; stitch ¼" on each side of the marked line as shown in Figure 1.

Figure 1

Charming Ohio Star Throw
Placement Diagram 54" x 54"

4. Cut apart on the marked line; press seams toward B.

5. Restack the two A-B units, layering the A side of one unit with the B side of another unit as shown in Figure 2; draw a diagonal line from corner to corner to cross the original stitching as shown in Figure 3.

Figure 2 **Figure 3**

6. Stitch ¼" on each side of the marked line as shown in Figure 4; cut apart on the marked line to complete two A-B side units, again referring to Figure 4. Press seams toward B.

Figure 4

7. Repeat steps 3–6 with the remaining A and B squares to complete two more A-B side units.

8. Trim A-B side units to 3½" square, centering seams as shown in Figure 5.

Figure 5

9. Sew an A-B side unit to opposite sides of the D square to make the center row as shown in Figure 6; press seams toward D.

Figure 6

10. Sew a C square to each A side of an A-B side unit to make a top row as shown in Figure 7; repeat to make the bottom row. Press seams toward C squares.

Figure 7

11. Sew the rows to the top and bottom of the center row to complete one Ohio Star block referring to the block drawing; press seams away from the center row.

12. Repeat steps 1–11 to complete a total of 25 Ohio Star blocks.

Completing the Top

1. Join five Ohio Star blocks and six E strips to make a block row as shown in Figure 8; press seams toward E strips. Repeat to make five block rows.

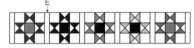

Figure 8

2. Join five E strips and four F squares and add a G square to each end to make an F sashing row as shown in Figure 9; press seams toward E strips. Repeat to make four F sashing rows.

Figure 9

3. Join five E strips and six G squares to make a G sashing row referring to Figure 10; press seams toward E strips. Repeat to make a second G sashing row.

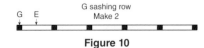

Figure 10

4. Join the block rows with the F sashing rows and add a G sashing row to the top and bottom to complete the quilt top referring to the Placement Diagram; press seams away from the block rows.

Finishing the Throw

1. Refer to Finishing Your Quilt on page 176 to sandwich, quilt and bind your throw to finish. ■

11

21" x 18"

Friends Together

Using fat quarters in two colors illustrates two friends, different but alike. This design makes a good signature quilt to give to a friend.

DESIGN BY JOHANNA WILSON

PROJECT NOTE

The sample project uses six each different navy and cream fat quarters. We have chosen to use five fat quarters each to simplify.

PROJECT SPECIFICATIONS

Skill Level: Beginner
Quilt Size: 32" x 44"
Block Size: 12" x 12" and 6" x 12"
Number of Blocks: 1 and 10

MATERIALS

- 1 fat quarter navy/brown print
- 5 different navy fat quarters (label 1–5)
- 5 different cream/tan fat quarters (label 1–5)
- ⅜ yard golden brown tonal
- ⅜ yard golden brown print
- ⅜ yard blue tonal for binding
- Batting 40" x 52"
- Backing 40" x 52"
- All-purpose thread to match fabrics
- Quilting thread
- Basic sewing tools and supplies

Cutting

1. Cut one 2⅞" x 21" strip from navy 1; subcut strip into seven 2⅞" squares. Cut each square in half on one diagonal to make 14 B triangles.

2. Repeat step 1 with cream/tan 1 to cut 14 C triangles.

3. Cut two 2½" x 2½" A squares from cream/tan 1.

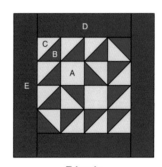

Friends
12" x 12" Block
Make 1

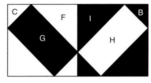

Together
6" x 12" Block
Make 5

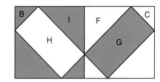

Reverse Together
6" x 12" Block
Make 5

4. Cut four 2⅞" x 2⅞" C squares, four 4⅞" x 4⅞" F squares and four 3⅜" x 6½" H rectangles from cream/tan 2; cut each C and F square in half on one diagonal to make eight each matching C and F triangles.

5. Cut four 2⅞" x 2⅞" B squares, four 4⅞" x 4⅞" I squares and four 3⅜" x 6½" G rectangles from navy 2; cut the B and I squares in half on one diagonal to make eight each matching B and I triangles.

6. From each cream/tan 3–5, cut two 2⅞" x 2⅞" C squares, two 4⅞" x 4⅞" F squares and two 3⅜" x 6½" H rectangles; cut each C and F square in half on one diagonal to make four C and four F triangles from each fabric.

7. From each navy 3–5, cut two 2⅞" x 2⅞" B squares, two 4⅞" x 4⅞" I squares and two 3⅜" x 6½" G rectangles; cut each B and I square in half on one diagonal to make four B and four I triangles from each fabric.

8. Cut two 2½" x 21" strips navy/brown print; subcut each strip into one 8½" D strip and one 12½" E strip.

9. Cut two 2½" by fabric width strips golden brown print; subcut strips into six 12½" J strips.

10. Cut two 2½" x 28½" K strips golden brown print.

11. Cut two 2½" x 40½" L strips and two 2½" x 32½" M strips golden brown tonal.

12. Cut four 2¼" by fabric width strips blue tonal for binding.

Completing the Friends Block

1. Select the navy 1 B triangles and the cream/tan 1 C triangles and A squares. Sew a B triangle to a C triangle along the diagonals to make a

Friends Together
Placement Diagram 32" x 44"

B-C unit as shown in Figure 1; press seam toward B. Repeat to make 14 B-C units.

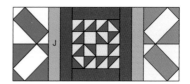

Figure 1

2. Arrange and join the B-C units with the A squares to make rows as shown in Figure 2; press seams in adjacent rows in opposite directions.

3. Join the rows as arranged to complete the center of the Friends block; press seams in one direction.

Figure 2

4. Sew a D strip to the top and bottom, and E strips to opposite sides to complete the Friends block; press seams toward D and E strips.

Completing the Together Blocks

1. From one cream/tan, select two each C and F triangles and one H rectangle; from one navy, select two each B and I triangles and one G rectangle.

2. Sew F to opposite long sides and C to the short ends of G to complete one cream unit, referring to the block drawing; press seams toward C and F. Repeat with B, I and H pieces to make one navy unit. Join the cream and navy units to complete one Together block.

3. Repeat steps 1 and 2 to complete five Together blocks and five Reverse Together blocks, using matching cream and navy pieces in each block referring to the block drawings, Placement Diagram and project photo for color placement and positioning of pieces.

Completing the Top

1. Join the Friends block with two J strips and one each Together and Reverse Together blocks to make the center row as shown in Figure 3; press seams toward J strips.

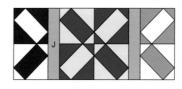

Figure 3

2. Join two each Together and Reverse Together blocks with two J strips to make the top row referring to Figure 4; press seams toward J strips. Repeat to make the bottom row.

Figure 4

3. Join the rows with K strips referring to the Placement Diagram; press seams toward K strips.

4. Sew L strips to opposite long sides and M strips to the top and bottom of the pieced center; press seams toward L and M strips.

Completing the Quilt

1. Refer to Finishing Your Quilt on page 176 to sandwich, quilt and bind your quilt to finish. ■

30
10" x 10"

Dream Windows Nap Quilt

Stack your 10" squares and cut them into three pieces for a fast way to create a quilt that will carry your child into a world of sweet dreams.

DESIGN BY KARLA SCHULZ

PROJECT SPECIFICATIONS

Skill Level: Beginner
Project Size: 42½" x 61"
Block Size: 6½" x 8½"
Number of Blocks: 30

MATERIALS

- 30 coordinating 10" x 10" squares
- ¾ yard yellow dot
- 1 yard aqua print
- Batting 51" x 69"
- Backing 51" x 69"
- Neutral-color all-purpose thread
- Quilting thread
- Basic sewing tools and supplies

Cutting

1. Cut each one of the 30 coordinating 10" x 10" squares into the following referring to Figure 1: 2½" x 10" A rectangle, 2½" x 7½" B rectangle and 7½" x 7½" C square.

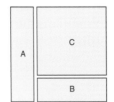

Figure 1

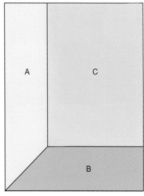

Dream Window
6½" x 8½" Block
Make 30

2. Trim each A rectangle to 2½" x 9⅜"; place the rectangle right side up and trim corner at a 45-degree angle as shown in Figure 2.

Figure 2   **Figure 3**

3. Trim each B rectangle to 2½" x 7⅜"; place the rectangle right side up and trim corner at a 45-degree angle as shown in Figure 3.

4. Cut each C square into a 5" x 7" rectangle as shown in Figure 4.

Figure 4

5. Cut two 5½" x 33" D strips aqua print.

6. Cut three 5½" by fabric width strips aqua print. Join the strips on short ends to make one long strip; press seams open. Subcut strip into two 51½" E strips.

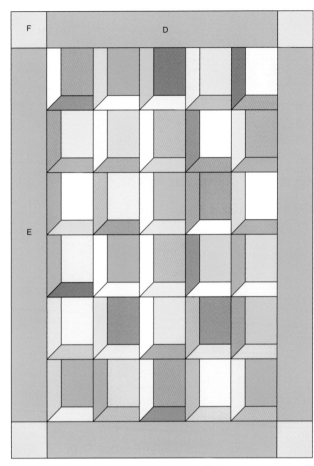

Dream Windows Nap Quilt
Placement Diagram 42½" x 61"

7. Cut one 5½" by fabric width strip yellow dot; subcut strip into four 5½" F squares.

8. Cut six 2¼" by fabric width strips yellow dot for binding.

Completing the Blocks

1. Mix and match the A, B and C pieces; select one of each piece to make a block set. Repeat to select 30 block sets.

2. To complete one block, sew B to C starting at the square edge and stopping at the seam line on the opposite edge as shown in Figure 5; secure seam at end. Press seam toward B.

Figure 5

3. Sew A to the B-C unit as in step 2, stopping at the B-C seam line as shown in Figure 6; press seam toward A.

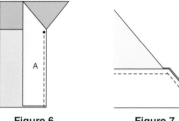

Figure 6   **Figure 7**

4. Fold C on the diagonal and match angled ends of A and B pieces and stitch, stopping stitching at the seam end as shown in Figure 7 to complete one Dream Window block. Press corner seam open.

5. Repeat steps 2–4 to complete 30 Dream Windows blocks.

Completing the Quilt Top

1. Arrange and join five blocks to make a row as shown in Figure 8; press seams in one direction. Repeat to make six rows, pressing seams in adjoining rows in opposite directions.

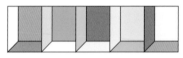

Figure 8

2. Join the rows, alternating pressed seams; press seams in one direction to complete the pieced center.

3. Sew an E strip to opposite long sides of the pieced center; press seams toward E strips.

4. Sew an F square to each end of each D strip; press seams toward D strips.

5. Sew the D-F strips to the top and bottom of the pieced center to complete the quilt top; press seams toward D-F strips.

Finishing the Quilt

1. Refer to Finishing Your Quilt on page 176 to sandwich, quilt and bind your quilt to finish. ■

Simple Log Cabin Throw

There isn't an easier way to make a Log Cabin quilt than to make one large block using strips that are already precut. This pattern is great for a baby quilt or a quick throw for a college student.

DESIGN BY TRACI GARNER

PROJECT SPECIFICATIONS

Skill Level: Beginner
Project Size: 42" x 58"

MATERIALS

- At least 40 each coordinating light and dark 2½" by fabric width strips—including 2 strips each 6 light and 5 dark
- ⅔ yard red solid or coordinating fabric for center square and binding
- Batting 50" x 66"
- Backing 50" x 66"
- Neutral-color all-purpose thread
- Quilting thread
- Basic sewing tools and supplies

Cutting

1. Cut one 4½" x 4½" A square red solid.

2. Cut six 2¼" by fabric width strips red solid for binding.

Completing the Quilt Top

1. Separate the 2½"-wide strips into light and dark values.

2. Sew a light strip to the A square as shown in Figure 1; trim the strip even with A and press the strip to the right side with seam toward the strip.

Figure 1

3. Turn the stitched unit a quarter turn counterclockwise; sew the remainder of the light strip to the A square as shown in Figure 2. Trim the strip even with A and press the strip to the right side with seam toward the strip.

Figure 2

4. Repeat steps 2 and 3 with a dark strip as shown in Figure 3 to complete one round of strips around the A square.

Figure 3

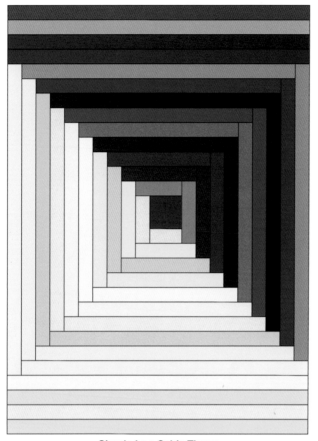

Simple Log Cabin Throw
Placement Diagram 42" x 58"

5. Continue in this manner, adding light strips to the light side and dark strips to the dark side, until you have added a total of 10 rounds on each light side and nine rounds on each dark side of A as shown in Figure 4. Note that you should use the same fabric on each light and dark round, so more than one strip of each fabric is required to complete the larger rounds. **Note:** *The first four rounds of each light and dark can be completed with just one fabric-width strip. Two same-color fabric-width strips are required for each of the remaining rounds. Periodically you may need to square up the unit using a rotary cutter and mat. For example, after adding four strips to each side of the A square, the stitched square should measure 21" square.*

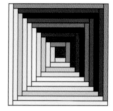

Figure 4

6. Select four light and four dark strips. Sew the light strips to the bottom and the dark strips to the top of the pieced unit; press seams toward strips. **Note:** *Because fabric widths vary, the last top and bottom strips to be added may or may not be long enough to fit. Measure the quilt top before adding the last round of strips and adjust as necessary.*

Finishing the Quilt

1. Refer to Finishing Your Quilt on page 176 to sandwich, quilt and bind your quilt to finish. ■

Quick Gifts

Create quilted gifts for family and friends in less time by using precut fabric packs. In this chapter, you'll discover eight gifts to make—a shoulder bag, tote bag, wallet, pillow, runner, apron, dog coat, wall quilt and even a pattern for making your own gift wrap. It's easier than ever to share your love of quilting with others.

Blissful Bag

Outside and inside pockets make this a handy bag to carry. Using fabric strips makes it quick to complete; it's so quick, in fact, that you'll want to make one for all your quilting friends.

DESIGN BY CAROLYN S. VAGTS

PROJECT NOTES

One package of 2½-inch strips yields enough strips to make four of these shoulder bags.

PROJECT SPECIFICATIONS

Skill Level: Beginner
Bag Size: Approximately 14" x 9" x 2" excluding handle

MATERIALS

- 10–2½" x 42" batik strips
- ¾ yard coordinating batik for lining
- ¾ yard fusible fleece
- Neutral-color all-purpose thread
- 1 large button
- Safety pin
- Basic sewing tools and supplies

Cutting

1. Prepare templates for the bag and outer pocket using the pattern given. *Note: The bag template is made using the whole pattern given. The outer pocket template is made using the smaller section marked on the bag pattern.* Cut lining and fusible fleece pieces as directed on pattern.

2. Cut one 7" x 6½" rectangle each coordinating batik and fusible fleece for inner pocket lining.

3. Cut one 2½" by fabric width strip coordinating batik.

4. Cut one 5" x 28½" rectangle coordinating batik.

5. Cut one 2" x 28½" strip fusible fleece.

Completing the Bag

1. Select and join eight 2½" wide precut strips with right sides together along length to make a pieced strip; press seams in one direction.

2. Using the prepared template, cut two bag pieces, one outer pocket and one 7" x 6½" inner pocket from the pieced strip, aligning the red solid line on the bag patterns with the same seam line on the pieced strip when cutting each piece, referring to Figure 1.

3. Iron the fusible fleece bag, and outer and inner pocket pieces to the wrong side of the matching-size lining pieces. *Note: The 2½" x 28" fusible fleece strip will be used later.*

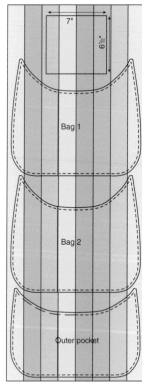

Figure 1

4. Layer the pieced outer pocket and the outer pocket lining with right sides together; sew along the long curved edge as shown in Figure 2.

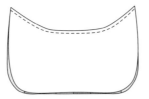

Figure 2

5. Turn the stitched outer pocket unit right side out; press stitched edge flat. Topstitch along the curved edge as shown in Figure 3.

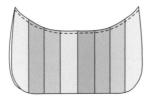

Figure 3

6. Place the outer pocket unit right side up on the right side of one of the bag pieces, aligning bottom edges as shown in Figure 4; pin to hold layers together.

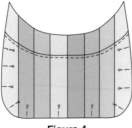

Figure 4

7. Using a scant ¼" seam, stitch the outer pocket to the bag piece to finish the bag front as shown in Figure 5.

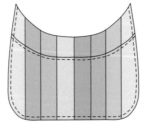

Figure 5

8. With right sides together, sew a 2½"-wide precut strip to the bag front for the gusset, starting at the top of one side and continuing around the bottom

curves and up to the other top side as shown in Figure 6. Press seam toward gusset strip.

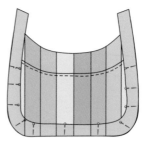

Figure 6

9. Add the bag back section to the opposite side of the gusset strip as in step 8, aligning the top edges of the bag back section with the top edges of the bag front, to complete the outer bag. Trim excess strip even with top of bag.

10. With right sides together, layer the pieced 7" x 6½" inner pocket with the prepared 7" x 6½" pocket lining and stitch around the sides leaving a 3" opening on one side for turning.

11. Turn right side out through opening; press edges flat and opening edges to the inside. Hand- or machine-stitch the opening closed.

12. Center and pin the inner pocket on the right side of one bag lining piece 2" down from the top edge as shown in Figure 7; stitch around three sides, leaving top edge open.

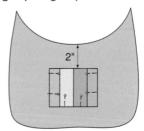

Figure 7

13. Assemble the lining as in steps 8 and 9, using the 2½" by fabric width strip coordinating batik for the gusset.

14. Lay the 5" x 28½" coordinating batik strip wrong side up; center the 2" x 28½" fusible fleece strip with the glue side down on the batik strip as shown in Figure 8.

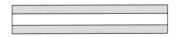

Figure 8

15. Fold the top of the fabric strip down until it is snug against the fusible fleece as shown in Figure 9; pin in place. Turn over and press so that the fleece is adhered to the fabric.

Figure 9

Figure 10

16. Fold ¼" to the wrong side on the remaining 28½" edge of the strip and press. Fold this edge over the fleece until it is snug; topstitch down the overlapped seam and ¼" from the opposite side to complete the handle as shown in Figure 10.

17. Cut a 7" piece off one end of the remaining 2½"-wide precut strip for the closure loop.

18. Fold the loop strip in half with right sides together along length; stitch along length. Turn right side out and press flat, centering seam on one side.

19. Cut a ½" x 7" piece of fusible fleece, and using a safety pin, pull it through the strip. Press loop strip to fuse fleece inside. Fold the strip in half to make a loop and stitch raw ends together.

20. Pin one end of the handle to the outside top edge of each end of the gusset strip as shown in Figure 11; machine-baste to hold in place.

Figure 11

21. Center the closure loop on the top edge of the right side of the back of the bag and machine-baste in place as shown in Figure 12.

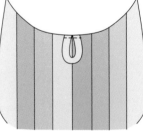

Figure 12

22. Insert the bag inside the lining with right sides together; pin top edges together matching gusset seams. Stitch all around top edge, leaving a 3" opening, referring to Figure 13.

Figure 13

23. Turn the bag right side out through the opening; press top edges flat at seams with lining on the inside. Turn in opening edges and hand-stitch closed.

24. Topstitch around top edge of bag ¼" from edge.

25. Center and sew the button 1½" down from the top edge of the bag front to finish as shown in Figure 14. ▮

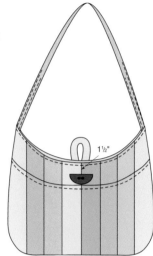

Figure 14

Blissful Bag
Placement Diagram Approximately 14" x 9" x 2" excluding handle

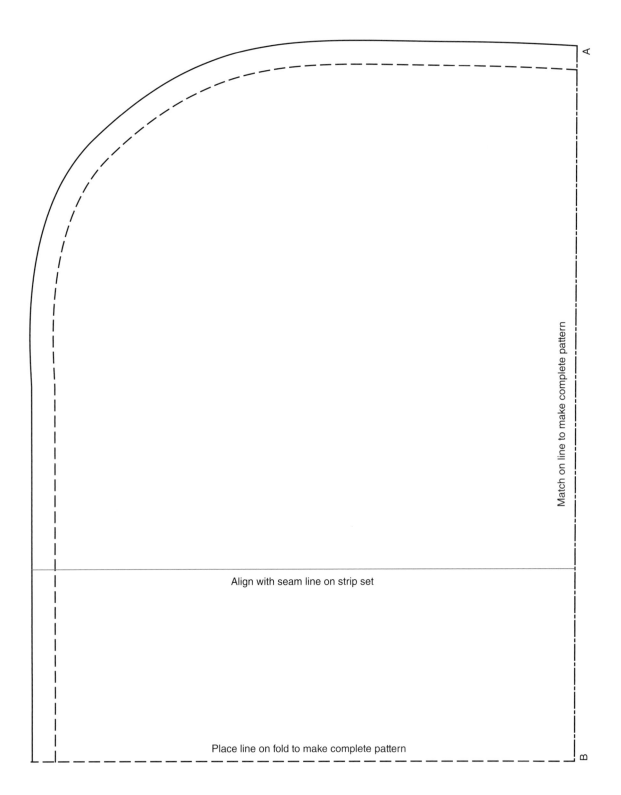

Match on line to make complete pattern

Align with seam line on strip set

Place line on fold to make complete pattern

A

B

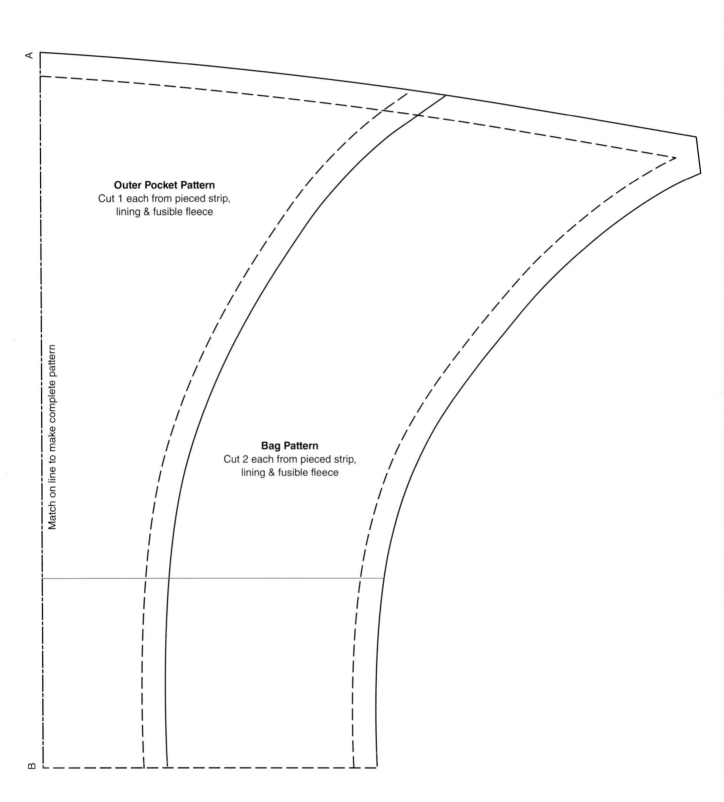

A

Outer Pocket Pattern
Cut 1 each from pieced strip,
lining & fusible fleece

Match on line to make complete pattern

Bag Pattern
Cut 2 each from pieced strip,
lining & fusible fleece

B

56
5" x 5"

Summer Sunflower Tote & Wallet

Step out in style this summer with a roomy bag featuring sunflower appliqués and a coordinating wallet with lots of pockets. This quick gift will delight all quilters.

DESIGNS BY CAROL ZENTGRAF

Summer Sunflower Tote

PROJECT SPECIFICATIONS

Skill Level: Intermediate
Tote Size: 15" x 18" x 3" excluding handles

MATERIALS

- 3 brown batik 5" x 5" squares
- 6 yellow/orange batik 5" x 5" squares
- 40 coordinating green batik 5" x 5" squares for A
- ½ yard green print
- ¾ yard yellow/orange batik
- 1¼ yards 22" cotton batting
- All-purpose thread to match lining
- Variegated machine-embroidery thread to coordinate with the yellow and brown batik fabrics
- ½ yard 1"-wide green grosgrain ribbon
- ¾ yard 18"-wide fusible web
- Lanyard clip with 1"-wide base
- 3" x 15" rectangle cardboard
- Permanent fabric adhesive
- Basic sewing tools and supplies

Preparation & Cutting

1. Using patterns given, trace 51 large petal pieces and three large sunflower centers onto the paper side of the fusible web leaving ½" between pieces when tracing; cut out shapes, leaving a margin around each one.

2. Fuse shapes to the wrong side of fabrics as directed on each piece for color; cut out shapes on traced lines. Remove paper backing.

3. Cut two 18½" x 21½" rectangles each yellow/orange batik for the bag lining and batting.

4. Cut a 5" x 17" rectangle yellow/orange batik to cover the cardboard strip.

5. Cut two 6" x 28" handle strips green print.

Completing the Tote

1. Arrange and join 20 A squares in five rows of four squares each; press seams in adjoining rows in opposite directions.

2. Join the rows to complete the tote front as shown in Figure 1; press seams in one direction.

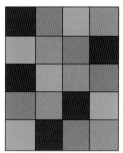

Figure 1

3. Repeat steps 1 and 2 to complete the tote back.

4. Trim the tote front and back sections to 18½" x 21½" as shown in Figure 2.

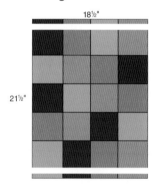

Figure 2

5. Referring to the project photo and Placement Diagram, and keeping the petals at least 3" from the tote front edges, arrange and fuse 17 large petals with one large flower center to make one large flower, overlapping petals as necessary. Repeat to fuse three large flowers.

6. Using the variegated thread, satin-stitch around edges of petals and then around the flower centers.

7. Baste a batting rectangle to the wrong side of the tote front and back sections.

8. Place the two sections right sides together and stitch along both sides and across the bottom as shown in Figure 3. Press seams open; do not turn right side out.

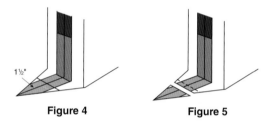

Figure 3

9. To shape the bottom of the bag, fold one bottom corner so the bottom and side seams are aligned and draw a line across the corner 1½" from the point as shown in Figure 4; stitch on the marked line as shown in Figure 5. Trim excess fabric ¼" from stitched line. Repeat on the opposite corner.

Figure 4   **Figure 5**

10. Turn right side out; press seams flat.

11. Insert the grosgrain ribbon through the base of the lanyard clip and baste the ribbon ends together.

12. With the clip centered on the ribbon, stitch across the ribbon at the base of the clip as shown in Figure 6.

Figure 6   **Figure 7**

13. Pin the ribbon ends to the right side of one lining panel 3½" from the top edge as shown in Figure 7.

14. Sew the lining rectangles together along the side and bottom seams, leaving an opening in the center of the bottom seam. Make square corners in the lining referring to step 9. Do not turn right side out.

15. Insert the tote inside the lining with right sides together, matching side seams. Stitch around the top edge as shown in Figure 8.

Figure 8   **Figure 9**

16. Turn right side out through the opening in the lining; turn in the seam at the opening ¼" and machine-stitch opening closed, close to the edge as shown in Figure 9.

17. Push lining inside the tote and press the top edge at the seam; topstitch ⅜" from top edge as shown in Figure 10.

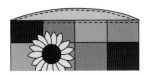

Figure 10   **Figure 11**

18. Fold 1½" along the top edge of the bag to the outside to make a cuff and press as shown in Figure 11.

19. To make handles, press one 6" x 28" handle strip in half along length with wrong sides together. Open the strip and fold the edges to meet at the center fold as shown in Figure 12; press.

Figure 12

20. Fold the strip in half again and topstitch along both long edges with thread to match lining; turn under ½" on each short end and stitch to complete one handle.

21. Repeat steps 19 and 20 to make a second handle.

22. Measure 4¼" from each side seam and pin handle ends down inside the bag 3½" with the turned edges against the lining and handles facing up. Topstitch handles in place at the top edge of the cuff using thread to match lining fabric as shown in Figure 13.

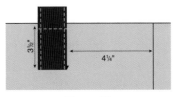

Figure 13

23. Lift the cuff and stitch across the handles again ½" below the first stitching as shown in Figure 14.

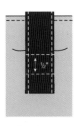

Figure 14

24. Wrap the yellow/orange batik rectangle around the cardboard rectangle and glue the ends to the underside with permanent fabric adhesive. Glue the covered cardboard into the bottom of the bag to finish.

Summer Sunflower Tote
Placement Diagram 15" x 18" x 3" excluding handles

Summer Sunflower Wallet

PROJECT SPECIFICATIONS

Skill Level: Intermediate
Wallet Size: 7½" x 9"

MATERIALS

- 5 coordinating green batik 5" x 5" A squares
- 1 yellow/orange batik 5" x 5" square
- 1 brown batik 5" x 5" square
- ⅜ yard yellow/orange batik
- 8" x 9½" rectangle cotton batting
- All-purpose thread to match fabrics
- Variegated machine-embroidery thread to coordinate with the yellow and brown batik fabrics
- Sew-on snap
- 7"-long green zipper
- 8" x 11" sheet fusible web
- Basic sewing tools and supplies

Cutting

1. Using patterns given, trace 8 small petal pieces and one small sunflower center onto the paper side of the fusible web leaving ½" between pieces when tracing; cut out shapes, leaving a margin around each one.

2. Fuse shapes to the wrong side of fabrics as directed on each piece for color; cut out shapes on traced lines. Remove paper backing.

3. Cut one 8" x 9½" rectangle yellow/orange batik for wallet inside.

4. Cut three 8" x 6" rectangles yellow/orange batik for inside pockets.

Completing the Wallet

1. Arrange and join two A squares to make a row; press seams in one direction. Repeat to make two rows. Join the rows with seams alternating in direction to make the wallet front as shown in Figure 15; press seam to one side.

 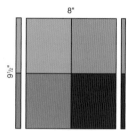

Figure 15	Figure 16

2. Trim the stitched unit to 8" x 9½" as shown in Figure 16.

3. Arrange and fuse the small flower motif in the center of one row of blocks, positioning the petals first and then the center. Satin-stitch pieces in place using the coordinating variegated thread.

4. Fold the remaining A square in half with right sides together; sew ends to make front pocket as shown in Figure 17. Turn right side out; press flat. Baste the open edges together.

Figure 17

5. Cut the zipper to 4½" long; stitch across the base of the zipper several times to prevent it from opening.

6. Sew the pocket to the right side of the zipper tape, matching the raw edges of the pocket with the outer edge of the zipper tape; fold the pocket down and topstitch the fold in place as shown in Figure 18.

Figure 18

7. Place the pocket on the wallet front so the bottom of the pocket is 1¼" from the center seam as shown in Figure 19. Flip the pocket up. Stitch the zipper tape in place on the wallet front.

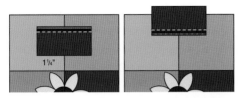

Figure 19

8. Fold the pocket down and stitch the side and bottom edges to the wallet front as shown in Figure 20.

9. Baste the batting rectangle to the wrong side of the wallet front.

Figure 20

10. Press the 8" x 6" inside pocket rectangles in half with wrong sides together along length. With the folded edge up and raw edges even, baste a pocket to one end of the 8" x 9½" wallet inside rectangle for the bills pocket as shown in Figure 21.

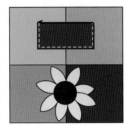

Figure 21

11. To make the credit-card pockets on the opposite end of the rectangle, place one pocket with the folded edge 3½" above the bottom edge of the rectangle with side edges even; baste ends in place.

12. Stitch across the pocket 2" from the folded edge. Place the remaining pocket on top of the first one, aligning the raw edges with the rectangle edges. Baste the side edges in place. Stitch across the pocket 2" from the folded edge. Sew a vertical line through the center of the pockets to finish the inside of the wallet as shown in Figure 22.

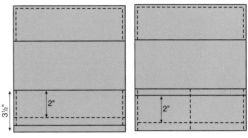

Figure 22

13. Place the wallet front right sides together with the inside of the wallet; stitch around edges, leaving a 3" opening in the bottom edge. Turn right side out through the opening; press edges flat. Press opening edges to the inside; slipstitch opening closed.

14. Center and sew the snap halves along the top and bottom edges to finish.

15. Clip to the tote with the lanyard to secure in the tote when in use. ■

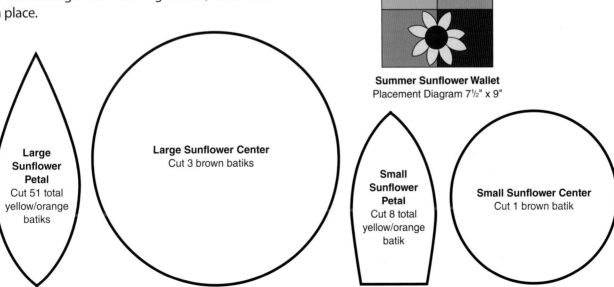

Summer Sunflower Wallet
Placement Diagram 7½" x 9"

Large Sunflower Petal
Cut 51 total yellow/orange batiks

Large Sunflower Center
Cut 3 brown batiks

Small Sunflower Petal
Cut 8 total yellow/orange batik

Small Sunflower Center
Cut 1 brown batik

Hibiscus Blooms Pillow

Add a tropical flair to your decor using 10-inch squares. The pillow top is quilted, and the center is tufted with buttons to add dimension to this colorful project.

DESIGN BY CAROL ZENTGRAF

13 10" x 10"

3 21" x 18"

PROJECT SPECIFICATIONS

Skill Level: Beginner
Pillow Size: 20" x 20"

MATERIALS

- 13 squares 10" x 10"—4 white solid, 4 hot pink tonal, 2 orange tonal and 3 medium green tonal
- 1 fat quarter light green tonal
- 2 fat quarters green print for backing
- ¾ yard muslin
- 24" x 24" low-loft batting
- All-purpose thread to match or contrast with fabrics
- Polyester fiberfill
- 1 package double-stick fusible web sheets— (5) 12" x 9" sheets in a package
- 3 (½") yellow buttons
- 3"-long doll-making needle
- Basic sewing tools and supplies

Cutting

1. Cut four 8½" x 8½" A squares white solid for background.

2. Cut four 2½" x 16½" B strips light green tonal.

3. Cut four 2½" x 2½" C squares from a 10" x 10" square medium green tonal.

4. Trace large petal, small petal and leaf shapes onto the paper side of the fusible web as directed on the patterns given, leaving ½" between the shapes.

5. Cut out shapes, leaving a margin around each one.

6. Fuse the shapes to the wrong side of the 10" x 10" squares as directed on patterns for color and number to cut. Cut out shapes on traced lines; remove paper backing.

7. Cut two 10½" x 20½" backing rectangles green print.

8. Cut a 24" x 24" square muslin for lining.

Completing the Pillow Top

1. Join the four A squares to make a 16½" x 16½" background square as shown in Figure 1.

Figure 1

2. Sew a B strip to opposite sides of the A square; press seams toward B strips.

3. Sew a C square to each end of each remaining B strip; press seams toward B strips. Sew B/C strips to top and bottom of the A square; press seams toward strips.

4. Arrange the leaf shapes on the diagonal 1½" from each corner of the A square as shown in Figure 2. ***Note:*** *The double-stick fusible web allows you to reposition pieces making it easier to move pieces as necessary until the whole design is ready to fuse in place.*

1½"

Figure 2

5. Arrange two large petals on each side of each leaf referring to placement lines marked on the leaf pattern.

6. Arrange the small petals in the center of the large petals referring to pattern for positioning.

7. When satisfied with the placement of all pieces, fuse shapes in place.

Finishing the Pillow

1. Sandwich the batting square between the fused pillow top and muslin square; pin or baste layers together.

2. Set your machine for free-motion stitching, and using a contrasting thread, stitch radiating lines from the center of the pillow to a little beyond the center of each small petal referring to Figure 3.

Figure 3

3. Using a regular straight stitch, stitch veins in the leaves and the corner squares with contrasting thread. Stitch ½" inside the outer edges of each large petal with thread to match fabric.

4. Using a close zigzag stitch and thread to match fabrics, sew around edges of the small and large petals. Repeat on the edges of the leaves using contrasting thread.

5. Trim batting and backing edges even with pillow top.

6. Join the two 10½" x 20½" rectangles on the 20½" edges to make the pillow back; press seam open.

7. Place the pillow back right sides together with the appliquéd pillow top; stitch all around, leaving a 4" opening on one side. Turn right side out through the opening; press edges flat.

8. Stuff fiberfill inside pillow through the opening until satisfied with the loft; turn in opening edges ¼" and hand-stitch opening closed.

9. To tuft the center, thread the 3"-long doll-making needle with a long length of doubled thread; knot the ends together and stitch though the center of the pillow from the back side to the front. Stitch through the holes of one button, and then through the center of the pillow to the back, pulling to indent the center of the pillow.

10. Without cutting the thread, repeat step 9 to sew the two remaining buttons in place; knot the thread securely on the back side of the pillow to finish. ■

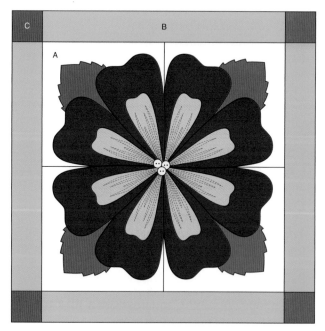

Hibiscus Blooms Pillow
Placement Diagram 20" x 20"

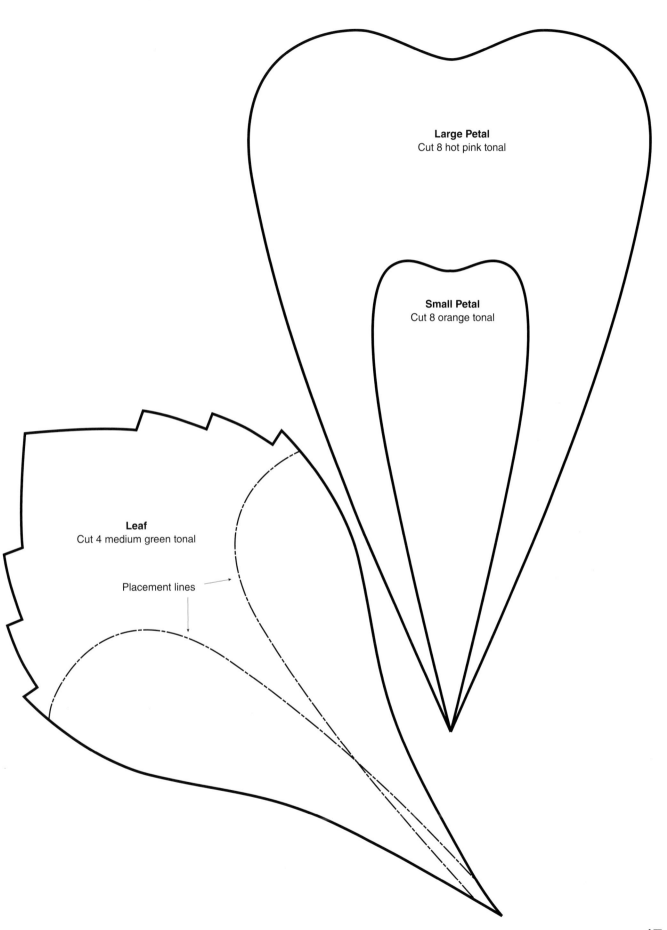

Large Petal
Cut 8 hot pink tonal

Small Petal
Cut 8 orange tonal

Leaf
Cut 4 medium green tonal

Placement lines

Quilt-As-You-Go Doggie Coat

Use leftover precut 2½-inch strips to make your dog this warm, snuggly coat for cold weather. It's a gift any dog owner will love.

DESIGN BY CHRISTINE SCHULTZ

PROJECT NOTE

The instructions are given to make a dog coat for a small-size dog, but the sample itself was made to fit a medium-size dog. The pattern is given to make a small-, medium- or large-size coat.

PROJECT SPECIFICATIONS

Skill Level: Intermediate
Coat Size: Small

MATERIALS

- 1 strip 2½" x 42" each of the following batiks: pine green with brown (1), dark pine green (2), light pine green (3), kelly green (4), grass green (5), lime green (6 and 8), olive green (7), orange (9 and center strip) and yellow (10)
- ⅔ yard Polar fleece
- Neutral-color all-purpose thread
- 3" hook-and-loop tape
- 2 (¾") shank buttons
- 6" narrow elastic
- Basic sewing tools and supplies

Cutting

1. Cut two 14"-long strips pine green with brown for strip 1.

2. Cut two 12"-long strips each dark pine green for strip 2 and olive green for strip 7.

3. Cut two 10"-long strips each light pine green for strip 3 and kelly green for strip 4.

4. Cut two 8"-long strips grass green for strip 5.

5. Cut two 5"-long strips (strip 6) and two 9"-long strips (strip 8) lime green.

6. Cut one 16"-long strip (center) and two 8"-long strips (strip 9) orange.

7. Cut two 6"-long strips yellow for strip 10.

Completing the Doggie Coat

Note: *When strip piecing, use ¼" seams. When assembling the coat, use ½" seams. Trim seams if necessary to reduce bulk at curves before turning right side out to topstitch.*

1. Enlarge the pattern pieces given 200 percent to make full-size patterns. Transfer all notes and grain lines. **Note:** *There are separate cutting lines for the fleece lining, batting half coats and the strip-pieced coat.*

2. Cut one coat lining, two collars and two belly bands from the Polar fleece. Cut two half coats from batting. Refer to patterns for placement and cutting lines.

3. Draw placement lines for strip 1 on the half-coat batting pieces.

4. Lay strip 1 in place on one half-coat batting piece; place strip 2 right sides together on strip 1.

Stitch with ¼" seam as shown in Figure 1; press strip 2 to the right side. Repeat with strips 3–6. Repeat with strips 7–10 on the other end of the coat batting piece to complete one side of the pieced coat referring to Figure 2.

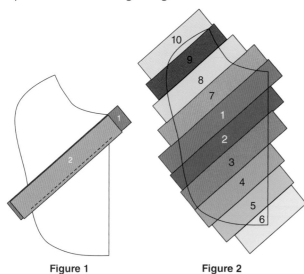

Figure 1

Figure 2

5. Repeat step 4 with the remaining half-coat batting piece to make a reverse side of the pieced coat referring to Figure 3.

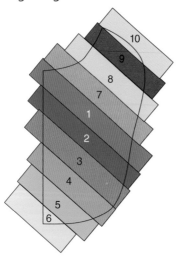

Figure 3

6. Trim the pieced half-coat sections to match pattern.

7. Fold the 16"-long orange center strip in half along length with wrong sides together. Pin in place along the center edge of one of the pieced half-coat sections with raw edges aligned as shown in Figure 4.

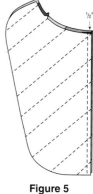

Figure 4

Figure 5

8. Place the second pieced coat section right sides together on top of the pinned strip, matching edges. Stitch the sections together with a ½" seam as shown in Figure 5.

9. When stitching is complete, open the two half-coat sections and press the orange center strip flat and centered over seam; topstitch close to the edge on each side of the strip as shown in Figure 6.

Figure 6

10. Pin-baste one collar piece to the top curved edge of the pieced coat, matching notches; sew in place as shown in Figure 7. Clip curves; press seam open.

Figure 7

11. Repeat step 10 with the second collar and the fleece lining piece.

12. Lay a belly-band piece and reverse belly-band piece right sides together; stitch around one short and two long sides of each layer with a ½" seam as shown in Figure 8.

Figure 8

13. Turn right side out, press and topstitch ¼" from edges as shown in Figure 9.

Figure 9

14. Sew a piece of hook tape to one belly band and a piece of loop tape to the second belly band as shown in Figure 10.

Figure 10

15. Pin the prepared belly bands in place with the wrong sides of the belly band facing the right side of the coat where indicated on pattern and referring to Figure 11.

16. Lay the fleece lining/collar and strip-pieced coat/collar/belly bands right sides together; sew around the outside as shown in Figure 12, leaving a 4" opening where indicated on pattern.

17. Turn the coat right side out through the opening; press edges flat. Turn opening edges to the inside and hand-stitch closed.

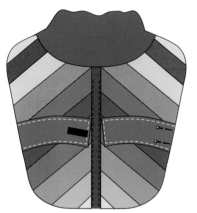

Figure 11

4"

Figure 12

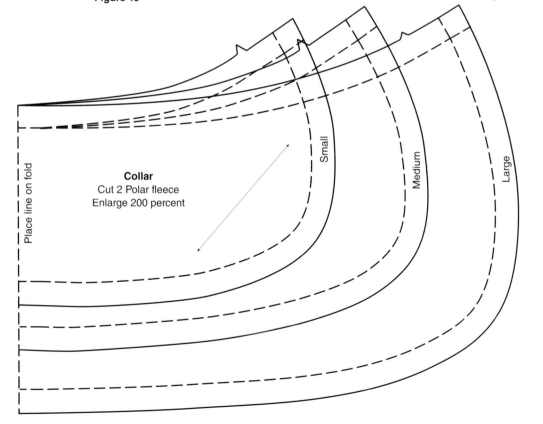

Place line on fold

Collar
Cut 2 Polar fleece
Enlarge 200 percent

Small

Medium

Large

18. Topstitch ⅜" all around edges of coat.

19. Sew one button on the coat at the collar seam front edge. Insert the end of the narrow elastic through the hole in the second button. Fold the elastic in half and knot one end. Make another knot halfway between the first knot and the button as shown in Figure 13. Sew a second button to the coat at the opposite collar seam on the front edge to finish. ■

Quilt-As-You-Go Doggie Coat
Placement Diagram
Medium Size

Figure 13

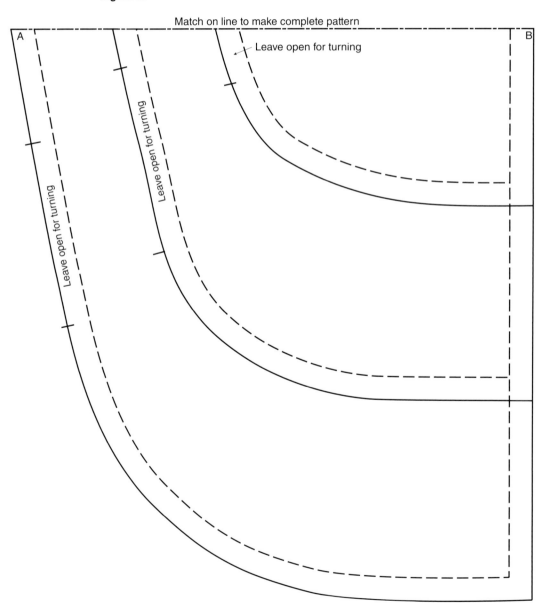

Match on line to make complete pattern

A

Leave open for turning

Leave open for turning

Leave open for turning

B

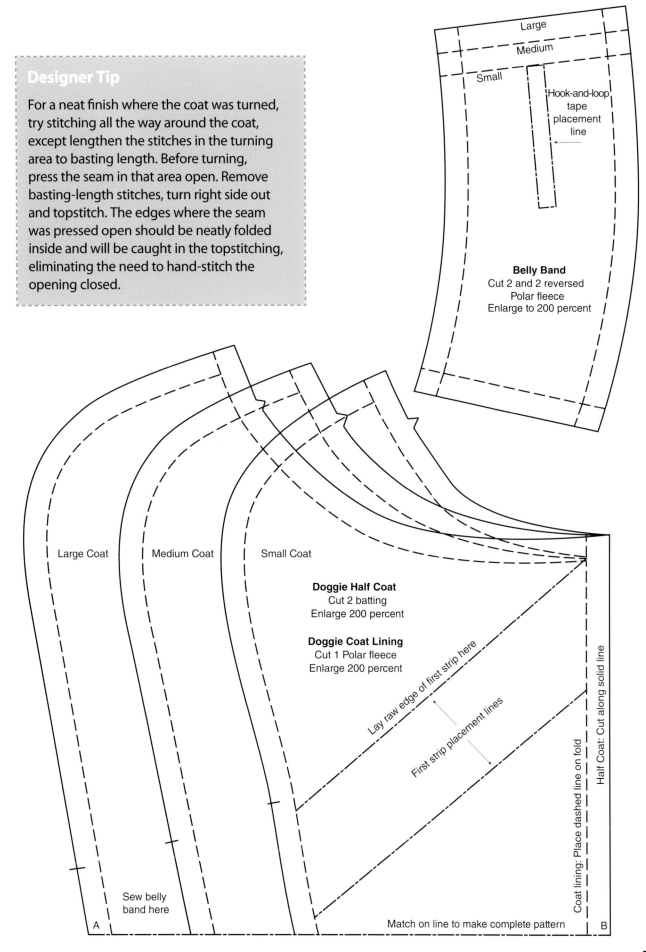

Designer Tip

For a neat finish where the coat was turned, try stitching all the way around the coat, except lengthen the stitches in the turning area to basting length. Before turning, press the seam in that area open. Remove basting-length stitches, turn right side out and topstitch. The edges where the seam was pressed open should be neatly folded inside and will be caught in the topstitching, eliminating the need to hand-stitch the opening closed.

Large

Medium

Small

Hook-and-loop tape placement line

Belly Band
Cut 2 and 2 reversed
Polar fleece
Enlarge to 200 percent

Large Coat

Medium Coat

Small Coat

Doggie Half Coat
Cut 2 batting
Enlarge 200 percent

Doggie Coat Lining
Cut 1 Polar fleece
Enlarge 200 percent

Lay raw edge of first strip here

First strip placement lines

Coat lining: Place dashed line on fold

Half Coat: Cut along solid line

Sew belly band here

A

Match on line to make complete pattern

B

Spring Nesting

Combine squares and strips for an easy wall quilt. The same block would make a lovely pillow to give as a quick gift.

DESIGN BY WENDY SHEPPARD

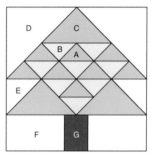

Nesting Tree
9½" x 9½" Block
Make 1

PROJECT SPECIFICATIONS

Skill Level: Beginner
Quilt Size: 20½" x 20½"
Block Size: 9½" x 9½"
Number of Blocks: 1

MATERIALS

- 1 (2½" x 42") strip each white-with-pink dots, and green, green butterfly, green leaf, pink leaf, pink butterfly, blue leaf and blue prints
- 3 (2½" x 42") strips blue leaf print for binding
- 1 (10" x 10") square each white and green prints, and red, brown and green dots
- Batting 28" x 28"
- Backing 28" x 28"
- White, green and brown all-purpose thread
- Quilting thread
- 8" x 8" square fusible web
- Basic sewing tools and supplies

Cutting

1. From the 10" x 10" square white print, cut one 5⅝" x 5⅝" square (D), two 2⅞" x 4½" rectangles (F) and one 3¼" x 3¼" square (E). Cut each of the D and E squares in half on one diagonal to make two each D and E triangles.

2. From the 10" x 10" square brown dot, cut one 2" x 2⅞" G rectangle. Set aside remainder for bird appliqué.

3. From the 10" x 10" square green dot, cut one 6" x 6" square (C) and two 3⅝" x 3⅝" squares (A). Cut the C square on both diagonals to make four C triangles; discard one. Cut each A square on both diagonals to make eight A triangles.

4. From the 10" x 10" square green print, cut two 3⅝" x 3⅝" squares (B); cut each square on both diagonals to make eight B triangles.

5. Cut four 1½" x 10" H strips from the 2½" x 42" strip white-with-pink dots.

6. Cut four 1½" x 1½" I squares from the 2½" x 42" strip blue print.

7. Cut one 2" x 12" J strip and one 2" x 15" L strip from the 2½" x 42" strip pink leaf print.

8. Cut one 2" x 12" K strip and one 2" x 15" M strip from the 2½" x 42" strip green print.

9. Cut one 2" x 15" N strip and one 2" x 18" Q strip from the 2½" x 42" strip green butterfly print.

10. Cut one 2" x 15" O strip and one 2" x 18" P strip from the 2½" x 42" strip pink butterfly print.

11. Cut two 2" x 18" R strips from the 2½" x 42" strip blue leaf print.

12. Cut two 2" x 21" S strips from the 2½" x 42" strip green leaf print.

13. Trace the bird motif pieces onto the paper side of the fusible web leaving ½" between shapes; cut out shapes leaving a margin around each one.

14. Fuse shapes to the wrong side of fabrics as marked on pieces. Cut out shapes on traced lines; remove paper backing.

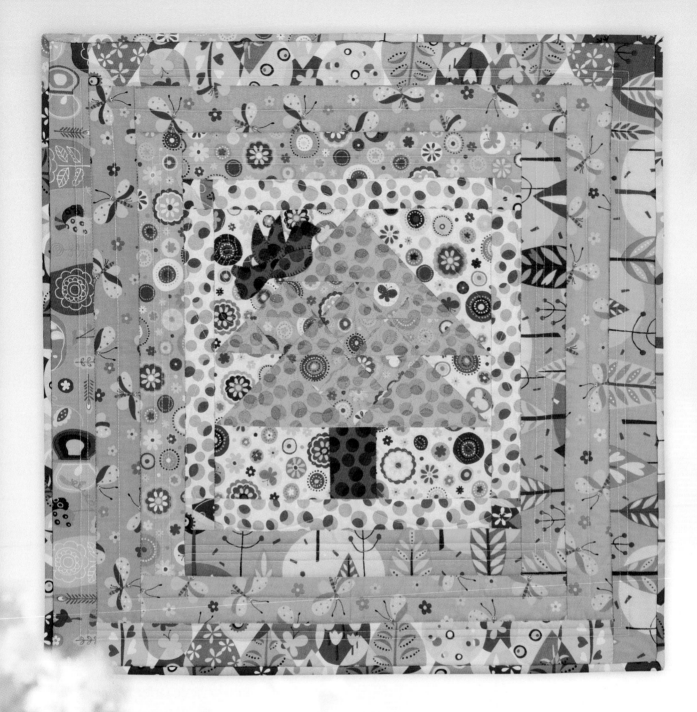

Completing the Block

1. Join two B and three A triangles to make a row referring to Figure 1; press seams toward A triangles.

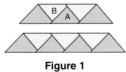

Figure 1

2. Repeat step 1 with three B and four A triangles to make a row, again referring to Figure 1.

3. Join the two rows and add a C triangle to the B side; add a D triangle to each side of the A-B-C unit to complete the top part of the tree as shown in Figure 2. Press seams toward C and then D.

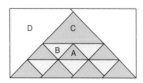

Figure 2

4. Sew A to B along the diagonal and add a B triangle to each remaining A side as shown in Figure 3. Press seams away from A.

Figure 3 **Figure 4**

5. Sew C to opposite sides of the A-B unit and add E to the C ends to complete the bottom of the tree as shown in Figure 4; press seams toward C and then E.

6. Sew G between two F rectangles to make the tree base as shown in Figure 5. Press seams toward G.

Figure 5

7. Join the three tree sections referring to Figure 6 to complete the Nesting Tree block; press seams toward the tree base.

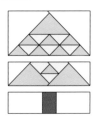

Figure 6

Spring Nesting
Placement Diagram 20½" x 20½"

Completing the Appliqué

1. Arrange and fuse the bird pieces in numerical order on the edge of the C and D pieces referring to the pattern and the Placement Diagram for positioning.

2. Using brown thread and a machine blanket stitch, stitch around each shape.

Completing the Top

1. Sew an H strip to opposite sides of the appliquéd block; press seams toward H. Sew an I square to each end of each remaining H strip; press seams toward H. Sew the H-I strips to the top and bottom of the appliquéd block.

2. Referring to the Placement Diagram, sew the J strip to the bottom, the K strip to top, the M strip to the left side edge and the L strip to the right side edge of the pieced center; press seams toward strips as added.

3. Repeat step 2 with N, O, P and Q strips.

4. Sew the R strips to the top and bottom and the S strips to the left and right side edges to complete the quilt top.

Finishing the Quilt

1. Refer to Finishing Your Quilt on page 176 to sandwich, quilt and bind your quilt to finish. *Note: Straight-line quilting, though considered simple and straightforward, can create an interesting look. Most of this quilt is quilted with straight lines to give a sharp contrast to the dense feather quilting in the tree.* ■

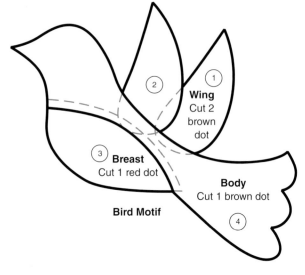

Bird Motif

Fresh Furoshiki Fabric Gift Wrap

Furoshiki is the ancient art of using a simple square of fabric and a few folds, twists and knots to make beautiful gift wrappings. There's no tape or ribbon to look for and nothing to throw away. The wrap is a valued part of the gift which the recipient can use as a table topper or reuse as a gift wrap.

DESIGN BY SUSAN FLETCHER

PROJECT SPECIFICATIONS

Skill Level: Beginner
Project Size: 20" x 20 to wrap a package
approximately 3½" x 5" x 3½"

MATERIALS

- 20 coordinating 1½" by fabric width strips
- 20½" x 20½" square coordinating organza
- Neutral-color all-purpose thread
- Basic sewing tools and supplies

Cutting

1. Trim each 1½"-wide strip to 20½" long.

2. Join the strips with right sides together along length to make a 20½" x 20½" strip-pieced square; press seams in one direction.

3. Place the organza square on top of the right side of the stitched square; pin and stitch all around, leaving a 3" opening in the center of one side.

4. Trim corners and turn right side out through the opening. Press flat from the pieced side to finish. Hand-stitch opening closed.

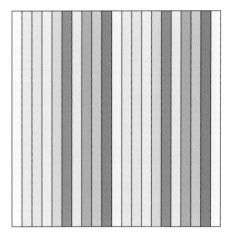

Fresh Furoshiki Fabric Gift Wrap
Placement Diagram 20" x 20"

How to Use Your Furoshiki Fabric Gift Wrap

1. Lay your wrap flat with the organza side facing up.

2. Place the gift in the center of the square, or if your gift is a square, situate on the diagonal.

3. Bring two opposite corners together over the gift and hold firmly where they meet above the gift, creating two rabbit ears above your hand. *Note: You can use an elastic band to hold the ears.*

4. Bring each of the remaining two corners together on one side of the rabbit ears, and then wrap them to the other side of the ears.

5. Tie in a tight half-knot.

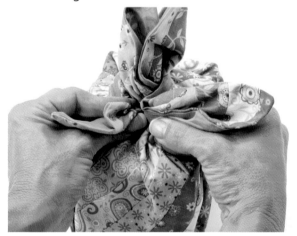

6. Bring the ends to the other side of the ears and tie again. ***Note:*** *If there is not enough length to bring to the other side, tie again over the half-knot.*

7. If you used an elastic band, snip it and pull it out. Then pull each of the ears upward very firmly. This will tighten the fabric against the gift, making the wrap prettier. You may want to tighten the knot now.

8. Tuck and tidy up around the sides as needed.

9. As an option to the standing ears, you could turn the points outward to display the organza fabric. ■

9

21" x 18"

French Bouquet

This miniature quilt is small in size, but big and beautiful in impact. Select nine fat quarters to make it happen, and give it to someone needing a touch of cheer.

DESIGN BY WENDY SHEPPARD

PROJECT NOTE

Before sandwiching the top for quilting, a monogram may be machine-embroidered in the center of the wreath, if desired. In the sample quilt, a detailed original-design quilt motif is quilted in the center instead of a monogram.

PROJECT SPECIFICATIONS

Skill Level: Intermediate
Quilt Size: 16" x 16"

MATERIALS

- 1 fat quarter cream solid
- 1 fat quarter green polka dot
- 1 fat quarter floral/green stripe
- 1 fat quarter each cream, green and salmon florals
- 1 fat quarter each floral/salmon stripe
- 1 fat quarter light green print
- 1 fat quarter salmon tonal
- Batting 21" x 21"
- Backing 21" x 21"
- Neutral-color all-purpose thread
- Tan silk thread
- ½ yard fusible web
- ⅜" bias bar
- 10" x 10" square of paper
- Water-erasable marker or pencil
- Black marker
- 22" of ¼"-wide fusible web
- Basic sewing tools and supplies

Cutting

1. Cut enough 1⅜"-wide bias strips from floral/salmon stripe and join to make 22" length for stem.

2. Cut one 10½" x 10½" A square cream solid.

3. Cut one 1½" x 21" strip green polka dot; subcut the strip into two 10½" B strips.

4. Cut two 1½" x 12½" C strips green polka dot.

5. Cut four 2¼" x 21" strips green polka dot for binding.

6. Cut two 2½" x 16½" E strips along the length of the floral/green stripe.

7. Cut two 2½" x 12½" D strips across the remaining width of the floral/green stripe.

8. Trace appliqué shapes onto the paper side of the fusible web referring to the full-size motif for number to cut, leaving ½" between pieces.

9. Cut out shapes, leaving a margin around each shape; fuse shapes to the wrong side of fabrics as directed on each piece for color. Cut out shapes on traced lines; remove paper backing.

Completing the Appliqué

1. To make the stem, fold the 1⅜"-wide length of bias along the length with wrong sides together; stitch a ¼" seam allowance along raw edge to make a tube as shown in Figure 1.

Figure 1

2. Insert the ⅜" bias bar inside the stitched tube with seam centered on one side as shown in Figure 2; press seam open. Remove bias bar.

Figure 2

3. Iron the ¼"-wide fusible web onto the wrong side of the stem strip; remove paper backing.

4. Fold the A square vertically and horizontally, and crease to mark centers. Repeat with the 10" square of paper.

5. Prepare a pattern for the full-size appliqué. Using a black marker, trace the pattern onto the 10" square of paper; matching the centers as shown in Figure 3.

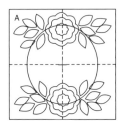

Figure 3

6. Center the drawing under the A square, matching center mark with creases on A as

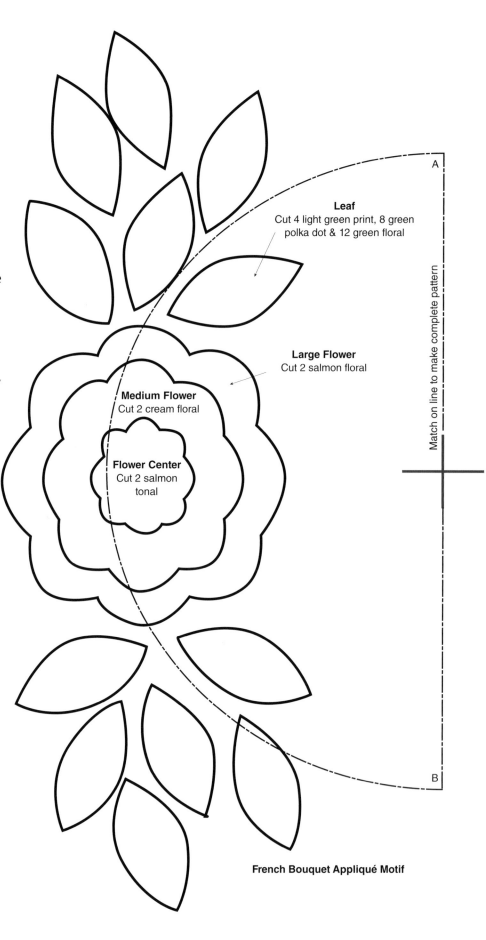

A

Match on line to make complete pattern

Leaf
Cut 4 light green print, 8 green polka dot & 12 green floral

Large Flower
Cut 2 salmon floral

Medium Flower
Cut 2 cream floral

Flower Center
Cut 2 salmon tonal

B

French Bouquet Appliqué Motif

Match on line to make complete pattern

A

B

shown in Figure 4; trace the design onto A using a water-erasable marker or pencil.

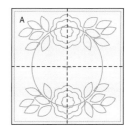

Figure 4

7. Center the prepared bias stem on the traced circle with the ends positioned to meet under one of the flower shapes; fuse in place. ***Note:*** *To reduce bulk, you may cut the bias in pieces to fit just under the flower pieces on each side before fusing as shown in Figure 5.*

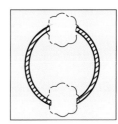

Figure 5

8. Using the tan silk thread and a very close and narrow blanket stitch, stitch the edges of the stem piece/pieces in place along each side.

9. Center, layer and fuse large and medium flowers and flower centers using the marked outline as guides for positioning.

10. Arrange and fuse leaf pieces using the marked outline as a guide for positioning.

11. Sew around each fused shape as in step 8 to complete the appliquéd center.

Completing the Top

1. Sew a B strip to the top and bottom, and C strips to opposite sides of the appliquéd center; press seams toward B and C strips.

2. Sew D strips to the top and bottom, and E strips to opposite sides of the appliquéd center to complete the quilt top; press seams toward D and E strips.

Finishing the Quilt

1. Transfer the quilting design given to the center of the appliquéd A square.

2. Prepare the finished top for quilting, quilt and bind referring to Finishing Your Quilt on page 176. ■

French Bouquet
Placement Diagram 16" x 16"

**Persian Feather
Quilting Design**

Celebrate With Precuts

Pull out all the stops and enjoy those special times of the year even more with designs stitched quickly from precut fabrics. In this chapter, you'll find 11 designs—a Christmas mantel quilt, Christmas place mats and napkins, Christmas stockings, an Americana lap quilt, Halloween runner and napkins, an autumn throw and a springtime wall quilt. You can start celebrating early.

3
21" x 18"

9
2½"

Jolly Jelly Stockings

No matter which way the strips run on the stockings you stitch, these fun Christmas stockings will make your celebration happy, festive and fun!

DESIGNS BY CAROL ZENTGRAF

PROJECT SPECIFICATIONS

Skill Level: Beginner
Stocking Size: Approximately 9" x 14" excluding hanging loop

MATERIALS

For 1 stocking:
- 9 strips total 2½" x 42" coordinating Christmas prints. ***Note:*** *Three stocking fronts can be cut from this 42" length.*
- 1 fat quarter coordinating polka dot for heel, toe and cuff
- 1 fat quarter coordinating print for backing
- 1 fat quarter coordinating print for lining
- All-purpose thread to match fabrics
- ¾ yard ½"-diameter coordinating ball fringe
- ¾"-diameter pompom
- 6" of ⅜"-wide red grosgrain ribbon
- 1½ yards ¼"-wide gimp trim for cuff, toe and heel, or ¾ yard for heel and toe only
- 1 sheet of double-stick fusible web
- Permanent fabric adhesive
- Basic sewing tools and supplies

Preparation & Cutting

1. Join the nine 2½" x 42" strips coordinating Christmas prints with right sides together along length to make a strip set; press seams in one direction.

2. Prepare patterns for stocking pieces using the full-size patterns given.

3. Lay the stocking pattern right side up on the strip set as shown in Figure 1. ***Note:*** *The stocking pattern may be placed diagonally or horizontally on the strip set. The orientation of the strips in each of the sample projects is different.*

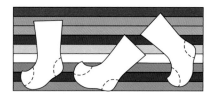

Figure 1

4. Reverse the stocking pattern and cut one backing piece from a coordinating fat quarter. ***Note:*** *If desired, you may cut the backing from the strip set.*

5. Fold a coordinating fat quarter along the 18" length; place the stocking pattern on top and cut out for lining as shown in Figure 2.

Figure 2

6. Cut four cuff pieces from the polka dot fat quarter.

7. Trace one each heel and toe shape onto the paper side of the fusible web, leaving ½" between pieces; cut out shapes leaving a margin around each one.

8. Fuse shapes to the wrong side of the polka dot fat quarter; cut out shapes on marked lines. Remove paper backing.

Completing the Stocking

1. Place the backing piece right sides together with the pieced stocking front; stitch, leaving top edge open. Trim seam and clip curves as shown in Figure 3. Turn right side out and press edges flat.

Figure 3

2. Repeat step 1 with the two lining pieces, except leave a 3" opening on the bottom of the stocking.

3. Join two cuff pieces on short ends to make outer cuff as shown in Figure 4; press seams open. Repeat with the remaining two cuff pieces to make the cuff lining.

Figure 4

4. With right sides together and side seams aligned, sew the outer cuff to the cuff lining along the bottom edge as shown in Figure 5. Clip into inverted seams and trim points, again referring to Figure 5.

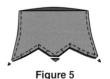

Figure 5

5. Turn the cuff unit right side out; press flat.

6. Pin and baste the ball fringe to the bottom edge of the cuff lining as shown in Figure 6; clip into ball fringe at inverted seams to allow it to lie flat.

Figure 6

7. Stitching from the outer cuff, sew the ball fringe in place ¼" from the edge of the cuff as shown in Figure 7.

Figure 7

8. With lining side of cuff unit against right side of stocking and matching side seams, pin and baste the stitched cuff unit around the top edge of the stitched stocking as shown in Figure 8.

Figure 8

9. Fold the piece of grosgrain ribbon in half to make a loop; baste to the top edge of the stocking at the side seam of the heel side as shown in Figure 9.

Figure 9

10. Matching side seams, upper edges and toe, pin the stocking inside the lining (right side of stocking against the right side of the lining); sew around top edge as shown in Figure 10.

Figure 10

11. Turn right side out through the opening in the bottom of the lining; press opening seam ¼" to the inside. Machine-stitch opening closed, close to the edge as shown in Figure 11.

Figure 11

12. Push the lining inside the stocking; press top edge along seam.

13. Arrange and fuse heel and toe pieces on the stocking front.

14. Use permanent fabric adhesive to glue gimp trim around the edges of the heel and toe shapes.

15. If desired, glue gimp trim around the lower edge of the cuff.

16. Glue a pompom to the tip of the toe piece to finish. ■

Jolly Jelly Stocking
Placement Diagram Approximately 9" x 14"
excluding hanging loop

Jolly Jelly Stocking
Placement Diagram Approximately 9" x 14"
excluding hanging loop

Jolly Jelly Stocking
Placement Diagram Approximately 9" x 14"
excluding hanging loop

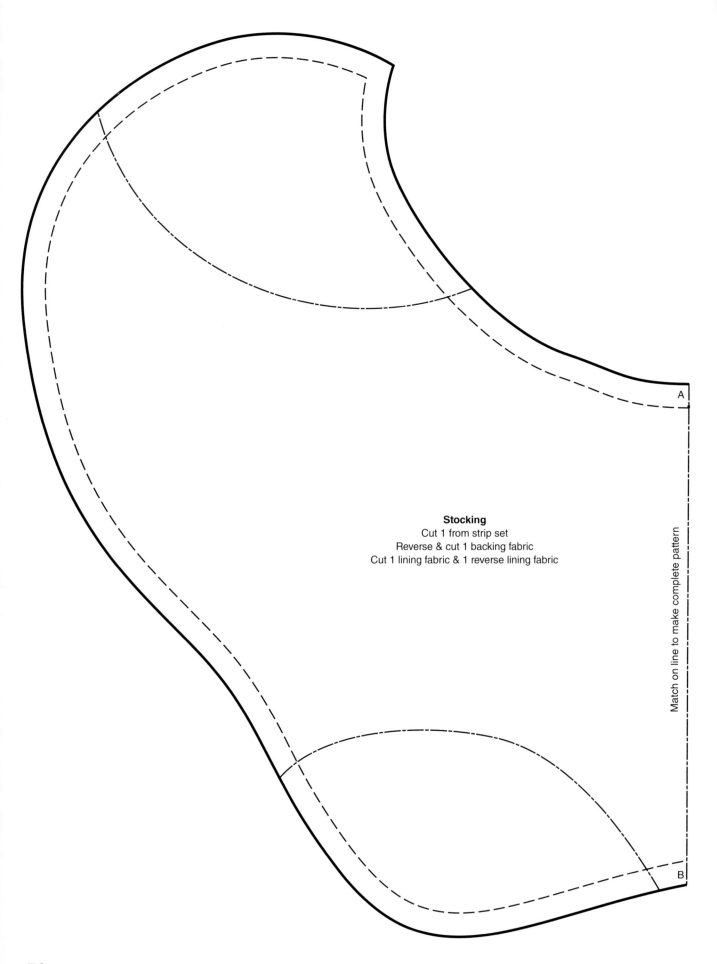

Stocking
Cut 1 from strip set
Reverse & cut 1 backing fabric
Cut 1 lining fabric & 1 reverse lining fabric

A

B

Match on line to make complete pattern

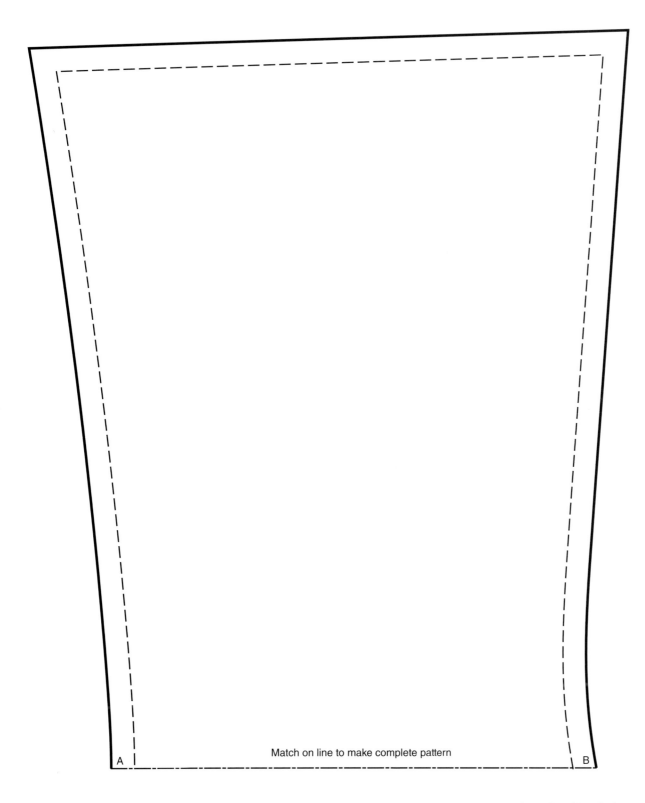

A

Match on line to make complete pattern

B

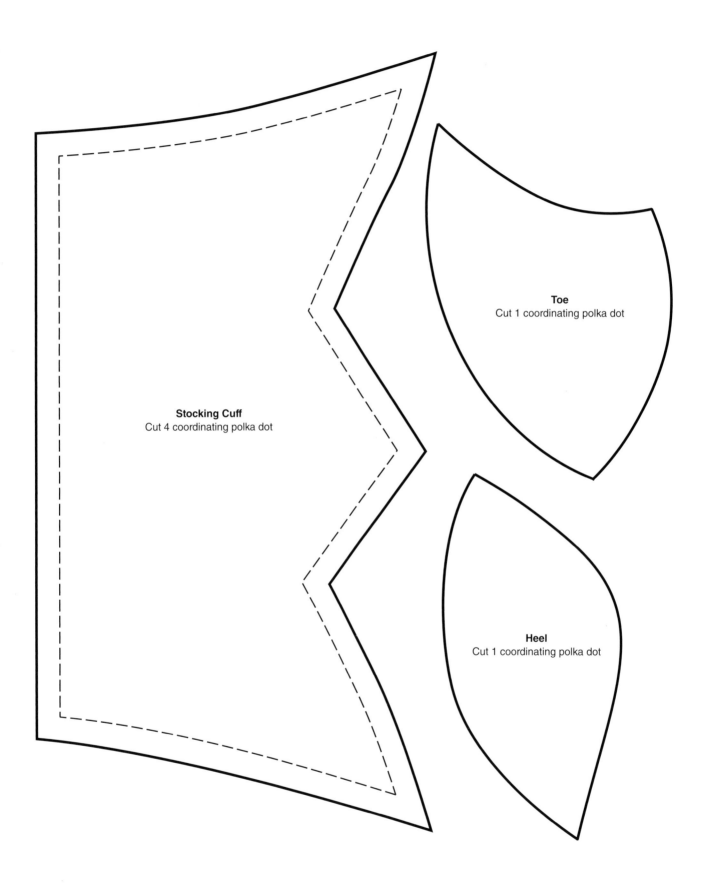

Stocking Cuff
Cut 4 coordinating polka dot

Toe
Cut 1 coordinating polka dot

Heel
Cut 1 coordinating polka dot

Americana Summer

Select a pack of 10-inch squares in your favorite colors to create a lovely lap quilt. We used red and blue fabrics for a quick summer picnic blanket or tablecloth. Add fusible circles to the sashing for a little pizzazz.

DESIGN BY CONNIE KAUFFMAN

PROJECT SPECIFICATIONS

Skill Level: Beginner
Quilt Size: 51¼" x 63⅛"

MATERIALS

- 6–9 each 10" x 10" squares red and blue prints
- 1 fat quarter red mottled
- ½ yard navy print
- ½ yard red print
- ⅝ yard light blue tonal
- ⅞ yard white tonal
- 1 yard navy mottled
- Batting 59" x 72"
- Backing 59" x 72"
- All-purpose thread to match fabrics
- Quilting thread
- 2 (9" x 12") sheets fusible web
- Basic sewing tools and supplies

Cutting

1. Cut the red and blue 10" x 10" squares on both diagonals to make at least 30 B triangles. **Note:** *The more squares you cut, the more variety you can create in your quilt top.*

2. Trim one blue and two red 10" x 10" squares to 5¼" x 5¼". Cut each square in half on one diagonal to make six C triangles.

3. Cut two 10" by fabric width strips white tonal; subcut strips into eight 10" squares. Cut each square on both diagonals to make 32 A triangles; discard two.

4. Cut one 5¼" by fabric width strip white tonal; subcut strip into three 5¼" squares. Cut each square in half on one diagonal to make six D triangles.

5. Cut six 2½" by fabric width strips light blue tonal. Join strips on short ends to make one long strip; press seams open. Subcut strip into five 48⅝" E strips.

6. Cut two 2½" x 40¾" G strips red print.

7. Cut three 2½" by fabric width strips red print. Join strips on short ends to make one long strip; press seams open. Subcut strip into two 48⅝" F strips.

8. Cut five 6" by fabric width strips navy mottled. Join strips on short ends to make one long strip; press seams open. Subcut strip into two 52⅝" H strips and two 51¾" I strips.

9. Cut six 2¼" by fabric width strips navy print for binding.

10. Trace the circle pattern given onto the paper side of the fusible web as directed on the pattern, leaving ½" between shapes.

11. Cut out shapes, leaving a margin around each one. Fuse shapes to the wrong side of the red mottled fat quarter.

12. Cut out shapes on traced lines; remove paper backing.

Completing the Top

1. Arrange five A triangles with five B triangles and one each C and D triangle to make an X row as shown in Figure 1; press seams toward B and C triangles. Repeat to make three X rows.

2. Repeat step 1 with the same number of A, B, C and D triangles, reversing the placement of triangles to make a Y row, again referring to Figure 1. Repeat to make three Y rows.

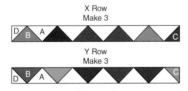

X Row
Make 3

Y Row
Make 3

Figure 1

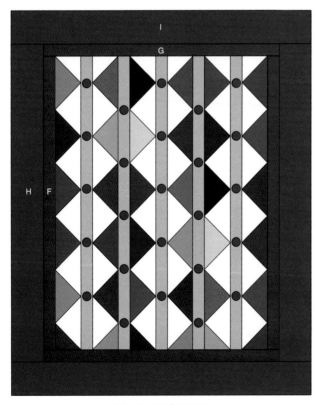

Americana Summer
Placement Diagram 51¼" x 63⅛"

3. Join one X row and one Y row with an E strip to make a double row as shown in Figure 2; repeat to make three double rows.

Figure 2

4. Join the double rows with the remaining E strips to complete the pieced center.

5. Arrange and fuse red mottled circles to E at the centers and points of the A triangles as shown in Figure 3.

Figure 3

6. Using thread to match the circles and a machine buttonhole stitch, sew around each circle.

7. Sew F strips to opposite long sides and G strips to the top and bottom of the pieced center; press seams toward F and G strips.

8. Sew H strips to opposite long sides and I strips to the top and bottom of the pieced center; press seams toward H and I strips to complete the quilt top.

Finishing the Throw

1. Refer to Finishing Your Quilt on page 176 to sandwich, quilt and bind your throw to finish. ■

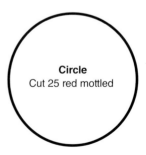

Circle
Cut 25 red mottled

Christmas Fun

This cheery mantel quilt can be used throughout the winter season. It is reversible, with Christmas prints on one side and tree appliqués on the reverse winter side.

DESIGN BY CHRIS MALONE

PROJECT SPECIFICATIONS

Skill Level: Beginner
Project Size: 49½" x 9" x 9½" drop

MATERIALS

- At least (25) 10" x 10" squares Christmas and winter prints with greens for trees
- Scrap brown tonal
- Batting 50" x 9½" and (5) 10" x 10" squares
- All-purpose thread to match fabrics
- Quilting thread
- ⅓ yard 18"-wide lightweight fusible web
- 15 (⁷⁄₁₆"-diameter) red buttons
- 5 (¾"-diameter) white snowflake buttons
- Walking foot (optional)
- Basic sewing tools and supplies

Cutting

1. Select 10 of the 10" x 10" squares for front and back A pieces. Prepare a pattern for the scallop. Fold each square in half, place scallop pattern on top, matching fold line on the scallop pattern to the fold on the square; trim as shown in Figure 1. ***Note:*** *If the print has a definite up-and-down pattern, trim the scallop at the bottom edge.*

Figure 1

2. Select four green or green/red squares for trees; cut each square into thirds to make a total of (12) 3⅓" x 10" B rectangles.

3. Cut (11) 10" x 10" squares into four 5" x 5" C squares each to total 44 C squares.

4. Trace the tree trunk shape onto the paper side of the fusible web as directed on pattern, leaving ½" between shapes; cut out shapes, leaving a margin around each one.

5. Fuse the paper shapes to the wrong side of the scrap of brown tonal; cut out shapes on traced lines. Remove paper backing.

Completing the Appliquéd Banners

1. Mix the 12 B rectangles into six sets of two each; join the two pieces in each set along the 10" sides to make six B units. Press seams open.

2. Trace the tree pattern five times onto the paper side of the fusible web, leaving ½" between shapes; cut out shapes, leaving a margin around each one.

3. Center and fuse a paper tree shape on the wrong side of five B units referring to Figure 2; cut out tree shapes on marked lines. Remove paper backing. Discard remaining B unit.

Figure 2

4. Center and fuse a tree and trunk shape on each A piece with scalloped edge at the bottom, tucking the trunk piece under the tree piece referring to Figure 3 and the pattern.

Figure 3

5. Using a machine blanket stitch and thread to match fabrics, stitch around each tree and trunk shape.

6. Place an appliquéd A right sides together with a plain A and pin to a 10" x 10" batting square; sew around sides and curved bottom, leaving the top straight edge open.

7. Trim batting away close to seam, clip the curves and turn right side out. Press edges flat.

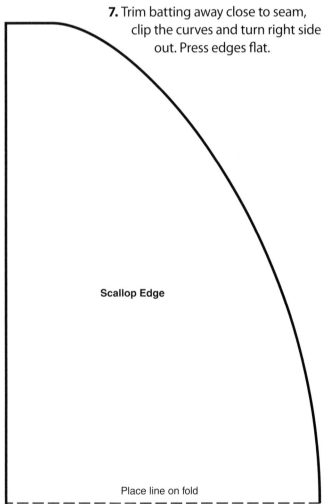

Scallop Edge

Place line on fold

8. Machine-stitch in the ditch around each tree motif using green thread. Stitch again ¼" away from the tree motif using cream thread. Topstitch the sides and bottom edges using cream thread to complete the appliquéd A banners.

Completing the Mantel Quilt

1. Divide the C squares in two sets of 22 squares each. Arrange each set into two rows of 11 squares each. Join the squares to make a row; press seams in one direction. Repeat to make a total of four rows, pressing seams in alternate directions.

2. Join two rows, matching seams, to make the top of the mantel section; press seams in one direction. Repeat to make the mantel back.

3. Place the mantel top right side up on a flat surface; evenly space the appliquéd banners right side down along the bottom edge of the mantel top with ⅜" at each end and ⅜"–½" between as shown in Figure 4.

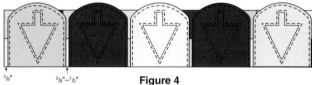

⅜"   ⅜"–½"   **Figure 4**

4. When satisfied with positioning, machine-baste in place.

5. Fold and pin each end banner back out of the way as shown in Figure 5. Pin the banner ends into the center of the mantel top.

Figure 5

6. Place the mantel back right side down on the basted/pinned mantel top; pin edges together.

7. Lay the pinned unit on top of the batting strip, matching straight edges. Using the walking foot, sew all around, leaving a 6" opening on the long edge opposite the basted edge. Trim batting close to seam, trim corners and turn right side out through the opening. Press edges flat.

8. Turn opening edges to the inside ¼"; hand-stitch closed.

9. Topstitch around each square of the mantel section using cream thread.

10. Sew three red buttons to each tree as marked on pattern, sewing through the top layer only. Sew a snowflake button to the top of each tree to finish. ■

Christmas Fun
Placement Diagram 49½" x 9" x 9½"

Centerline

Tree
Cut 5 from B units

Tree Trunk
Cut 5 brown tonal scrap

21" x 18"

Hooray for Holidays

Dress your holiday table with this fun set of place mats and napkins. Use a coordinated set of fat quarters and make them reversible.

DESIGN BY REEZE L. HANSON

PROJECT NOTES

The fabrics listed will make at least four place mats and four napkins. The instructions are written for making one of each.

PROJECT SPECIFICATIONS

Skill Level: Beginner
Place Mat Size: 17½" x 13½"
Napkin Size: 13½" x 13½"

MATERIALS

- 20 coordinating fat quarters
- Batting 22" x 18" thin batting for each place mat
- Neutral-color all-purpose thread
- Quilting thread
- Basting spray or safety pins
- Water-erasable marker
- Basic sewing tools and supplies

Cutting

1. Select eight coordinating fat quarters for one place mat and napkin set. Designate which fat quarter will be used for the A center, B ends, C pocket, D pocket edge, E binding and F backing; the remaining two fat quarters will be used for the napkin. *Note: You may mix and match fabrics to use the same fabric as the D fabric for binding or the backing may be cut from the remaining D fabric. Save all remaining fabric pieces to combine and use for more place mats.*

2. From the A fabric, cut one 14" x 14" A square.

3. From the B fabric, cut two 2½ " x 14" B rectangles.

4. From the C fabric, cut one 10" x 10" square; cut in half on one diagonal to make two C triangles.

5. From the D fabric, cut one 1½" x 15" D strip.

6. Cut and piece 2¼" bias strips from fabric E to make an 80"-long strip.

7. Cut one 14" x 14" square from each of the remaining fat quarters for napkin.

Completing the Place Mat

1. Sew a B strip to opposite ends of A; press seams toward B strips.

2. Mark diagonal crosshatch lines 1¾" apart on the A-B top using a water-erasable marker as shown in Figure 1.

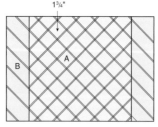

1¾"

Figure 1

3. Sandwich the batting between the A-B top and the F backing fat quarter with right sides out; apply basting spray or use safety pins to hold layers together.

4. Stitch on the marked lines; remove marker lines. *Note: A walking foot may be used on your machine to keep layers from shifting.*

5. Trim the backing and batting edges even with the A-B top.

6. Fold and press the 1½"-wide D strip in half with wrong sides together along length.

7. Pin the pressed D strip along the diagonal of a C triangle, matching raw edges as shown in Figure 2.

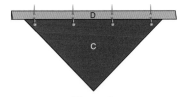

Figure 2

8. Place the second C triangle right sides together on top of the pinned C-D unit; stitch together along the long diagonal edge as shown in Figure 3.

Figure 3

9. Press one C to the wrong side, and D up and away from the C pieces and trim excess D to match C as shown in Figure 4.

Figure 4

10. Align the edges of the C-D pocket with one corner of the quilted A-B top and machine-baste in place as shown in Figure 5.

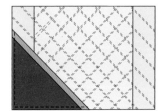

Figure 5

11. Join the binding strips on the short ends to make one long strip; fold with wrong sides together along length and press.

12. Pin the binding strip to the back side of the place mat; stitch in place, mitering corners and overlapping at the ends. *Note: Refer to Finishing Your Quilt on page 176 for a more thorough explanation of binding edges.*

13. Press the binding up and over to the top side of the place mat, enclosing raw edges.

14. Blind-stitch binding in place all around to finish the place mat.

Completing the Napkin

1. Place the two 14" x 14" napkin squares right sides together, aligning edges.

2. Stitch all around, leaving a 3" opening on one side.

3. Clip corners; turn right side out through the opening.

4. Press opening edges ¼" to the inside.

5. Topstitch layers together close to the edge, closing the opening at the same time.

6. Fold napkin as shown in Figure 6 and place inside the place mat pocket. ■

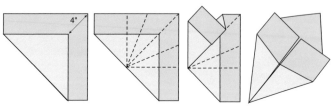

Figure 6

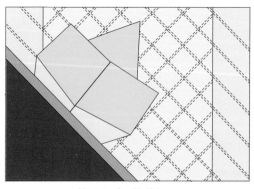

Hooray for Holidays
Placement Diagram 17½" x 13½"

Cheerful Blooms & Buttons

Use fat quarters in bright colors, and add rickrack and buttons for a touch of whimsy on this lovely floral quilt that will help you celebrate spring.

DESIGN BY AVIS SHIRER

PROJECT SPECIFICATIONS

Skill Level: Beginner
Quilt Size: 28" x 44"
Block Size: 4" x 12"
Number of Blocks: 15

MATERIALS

- 1 fat quarter each rose solid, pink plaid, blue mottled, green stripe and yellow print
- 1 fat quarter each deep rose and green tonals
- 1 fat quarter each 2 cream tonals
- ¼ yard rose/pink stripe
- ⅞ yard rose floral
- Batting 36" x 52"
- Backing 36" x 52"
- All-purpose thread to match fabrics and rickrack
- Green variegated thread
- Quilting thread
- 2 yards pale yellow jumbo rickrack
- 24 (½") dark pink buttons
- 1 yard fusible web
- Basic sewing tools and supplies

Cutting

1. Cut eight 4½" x 12½" total A rectangles from the two cream tonals.

2. Cut two 4½" x 21" strips rose solid; subcut strips into (14) 2½" B rectangles.

Flower
4" x 12" Block
Make 8

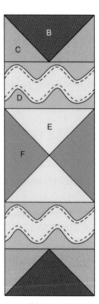

Rickrack
4" x 12" Block
Make 7

3. Cut four 2½" x 21" strips pink plaid; subcut strips into (28) 2½" C squares.

4. Cut two 4½" x 21" strips blue mottled; subcut strips into (14) 2½" D rectangles.

5. Cut one 5¼" x 21" strip each yellow print (E) and green stripe (F); subcut each strip into four 5¼" squares. Cut each square on both diagonals to make 16 each E and F triangles; discard two triangles each fabric.

6. Cut one 4¼" x 21" strip each yellow print (K) and green stripe (L); subcut each strip into two 4¼" squares. Cut each square on both diagonals to make eight each K and L triangles.

7. Cut three 1½" by fabric width strips rose/pink stripe; subcut one strip into two 20½" G strips. Trim remaining strips to make two 38½" H strips.

8. Cut two 3½" x 22½" I strips and two 3½" x 38½" J strips rose floral.

9. Cut four 2¼" by fabric width strips rose floral for binding.

10. Trace appliqué shapes onto the paper side of the fusible web as directed on patterns, leaving ½" between pieces. Cut out shapes, leaving a margin around each one.

11. Fuse shapes to the wrong side of fabrics as directed on each piece for color; cut out shapes on traced lines. Remove paper backing.

12. Cut the pale yellow jumbo rickrack into (14) 4½" lengths.

Completing the Flower Blocks

1. Fold each A rectangle in half vertically and horizontally to mark the centers.

2. To complete one Flower block, center and fuse the stem piece in place on A, matching the center mark on the stem and the creased center on A. Add the flower and leaf shapes referring to pattern and block drawing for positioning.

3. Using green variegated thread and a machine blanket stitch, stitch around the edges of the stem and leaves. Repeat on the flower using thread to match fabric.

4. Repeat steps 2 and 3 to complete eight Flower blocks.

Completing the Rickrack Blocks

1. Mark a diagonal line from corner to corner on the wrong side of each C square.

2. Place a C square right sides together on one corner of B and stitch on the marked line as shown in Figure 1; trim seam allowance to ¼" and press C to the right side, again referring to Figure 1.

Figure 1

3. Repeat step 2 on the opposite end of B to complete a B-C unit as shown in Figure 2.

Figure 2

4. Repeat steps 2 and 3 to complete 14 B-C units.

5. Join one E and one F on a short side to make an E-F unit as shown in Figure 3; press seam toward F. Repeat to make 14 E-F units.

Figure 3   **Figure 4**

6. Join two E-F units to complete an E-F square as shown in Figure 4; press seam to one side. Repeat to make seven E-F squares.

7. To complete one Rickrack block, sew a D rectangle to the E sides of an E-F square as shown in Figure 5; press seams toward D.

Figure 5

8. Sew a B-C unit to the D sides of the pieced unit as shown in Figure 6; press seams toward D.

Figure 6

9. Center and sew a 4½" length of pale yellow jumbo rickrack onto each D rectangle, sewing along curve on each edge of the rickrack with matching thread as shown in Figure 7.

Figure 7

10. Repeat steps 7–9 to complete a total of seven Rickrack blocks.

Completing the Quilt Top

1. Arrange and join three Flower blocks with two Rickrack blocks to make a row as shown in Figure 8; press seams toward Flower blocks. Repeat to make two rows.

2. Join three Rickrack blocks with two Flower blocks to make a row, again referring to Figure 8; press seams toward Flower blocks.

Make 2

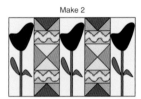

Make 1

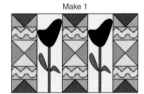

Figure 8

3. Join the rows referring to the Placement Diagram to complete the pieced center; press seams in one direction.

4. Sew a G strip to the top and bottom, and H strips to opposite long sides of the pieced center; press seams toward the G and H strips.

5. Sew a J strip to opposite long sides of the pieced center; press seams toward J strips.

6. Join one K and one L on a short side to make a K-L unit as shown in Figure 9; press seam toward L. Repeat to make eight K-L units.

Figure 9

7. Join two K-L units to complete a K-L square as shown in Figure 10; press seam to one side. Repeat to make four K-L squares.

Figure 10

8. Sew a K-L square to each end of each I strip, matching the L sides of the squares to the strips referring to the Placement Diagram for positioning; press seams toward I strips.

9. Sew the K-L/I strips to the top and bottom of the pieced center to complete the pieced top.

Finishing the Quilt

1. Refer to Finishing Your Quilt on page 176 to sandwich, quilt and bind your quilt to finish.

2. When quilting is complete, sew three dark pink buttons to each Flower block referring to the Placement Diagram and the quilt photo for positioning. ■

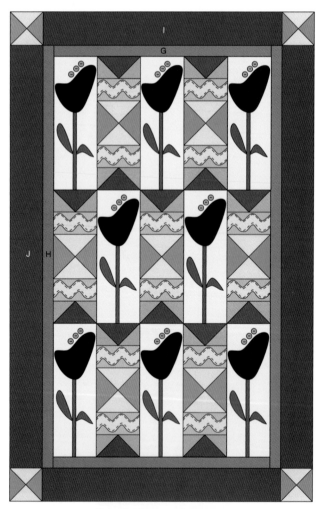

Cheerful Blooms & Buttons
Placement Diagram 28" x 44"

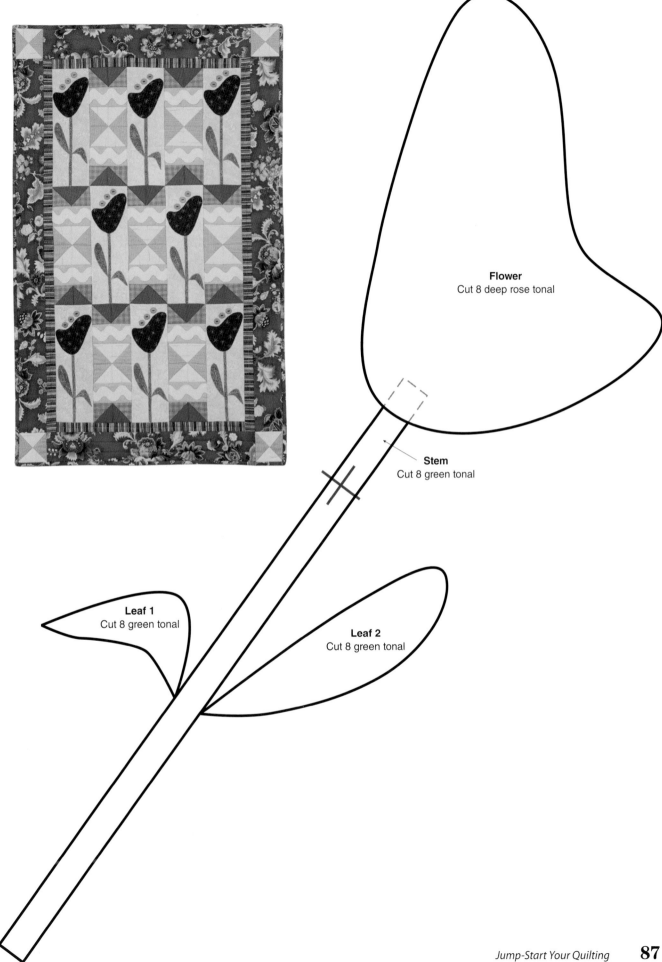

Flower
Cut 8 deep rose tonal

Stem
Cut 8 green tonal

Leaf 1
Cut 8 green tonal

Leaf 2
Cut 8 green tonal

Climbing Vines & Squares

Create a dynamic patchwork center to this throw by setting the 10-inch precut squares on point. Intertwining vines and leaves frame the patchwork.

DESIGN BY CHRIS MALONE

PROJECT SPECIFICATIONS

Skill Level: Beginner
Throw Size: 57½" x 57½"

MATERIALS

- 18 squares 10" x 10" total coordinating green, tan, dark and light blue, and brown prints and tonals
- ½ yard dark green print
- ¾ yard light green print
- ⅞ yard dark brown print
- 2¼ yards cream tonal
- Batting 66" x 66"
- Backing 66" x 66"
- All-purpose thread to match fabrics
- Quilting thread
- 13 (⅞") brown mottled buttons
- ⅜" and ½" pressing bars (optional)
- Basic sewing tools and supplies

Cutting

1. Cut one 14¾" by fabric width strip cream tonal; subcut strip into two 14¾" squares. Cut each square on both diagonals to make eight C triangles as shown in Figure 1.

2. Cut one 7⅝" by fabric width strip cream tonal; subcut strip into two 7⅝" squares. Cut each square in half on one diagonal to make four B triangles, again referring to Figure 1. Trim the remainder of the 7⅝" strip to 7½".

Figure 1

3. Cut five 7½" by fabric width strips cream tonal. Join these strips and the trimmed strip from step 2 on short ends to make one long strip; press seams open. Subcut strip into two 44" F strips and two 58" G strips.

4. Cut five 2" by fabric width strips dark brown print. Join strips on short ends to make one long strip; press seams open. Subcut strip into two 41" D strips and two 44" E strips.

5. Cut six 2¼" by fabric width strips dark brown print for binding.

6. Select 13 (10" x 10") A squares for quilt center; set aside. ***Note:*** *You will need one green, four blue, three brown and five tan squares to replicate the sample quilt.*

7. Cut a total of 190" of 1⅝"-wide H bias vine strips light green print.

8. Cut four 1⅜" x 15" I bias vine strips dark green print.

9. Prepare templates for the flower and leaf pieces using patterns given. Cut as directed on each piece using the remaining 10" x 10" squares and light green print, adding a ¼" seam allowance all around when cutting for hand appliqué. ***Note:*** *Four large leaf shapes will just fit on a 10" x 10" square, but be sure all four are positioned before cutting.*

Completing the Top

1. Arrange and join the A squares with the B and C triangles in diagonal rows as shown in Figure 2; press seams in adjoining rows in opposite directions.

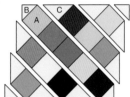

Figure 2

2. Join the rows to complete the pieced center; press seams in one direction.

3. Sew D strips to opposite sides and E strips to the top and bottom of the pieced center; press seams toward D and E strips.

4. Sew F strips to opposite sides and G strips to the top and bottom of the pieced center to complete the pieced top; press seams toward F and G strips.

Completing the Appliqué

1. Join the light green H bias strips with diagonal seams to make one long strip as shown in Figure 3; press seams open.

Figure 3

2. Trim strip to make two 65" lengths and four 13" lengths.

3. Fold each H and I bias strip in half with wrong sides together along length; stitch a scant ¼" seam down the length of each strip. Trim seam to ⅛". Press seams open with seams running down the center of the length as shown in Figure 4. **Note:** *If using pressing bars, use the ½" bar for the H strips and the ⅜" bar for the I strips. Insert bar in the strip, center seam and press open. Remove pressing bars.*

Figure 4

4. Referring to the Placement Diagram and project photo, arrange and pin the prepared 65" H vines, placing the center of each at opposite corners. Gently curve the vines. Arrange one 15" I vine on each side, tucking one end under the long H vine and bringing the other end over the D and E border strips. Arrange the 13" H vines near the ends of the 65" vines as shown, tucking one end under the long H vine. When satisfied with positioning, baste vine pieces in place.

5. Using thread to match vine fabrics, hand-appliqué vine pieces in place along both sides.

6. Turn under the seam allowance on each leaf and flower piece; baste in place.

7. Arrange and baste the leaves and flowers in place on the vines referring to the Placement Diagram and project photo for positioning.

8. Hand-appliqué flower and leaf pieces in place, being careful to make smooth curves and precise points when stitching.

Finishing the Quilt

1. Refer to Finishing Your Quilt on page 176 to sandwich, quilt and bind your throw. **Note:** *The quilt shown was machine-quilted using a walking*

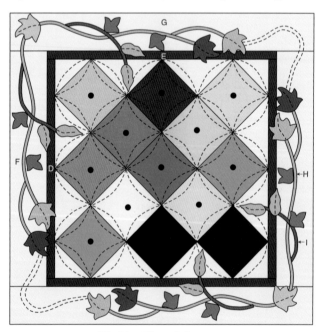

Climbing Vines & Squares
Placement Diagram 57½" x 57½"

foot, stitching in the ditch along all seams and around all appliqués. The two plain corners on the borders have a stitched continuation of the vine pattern and the leaves have a stitched center vein. Each A square a B and C triangle has a stitched curved line from corner to corner along each side as shown in Figure 5.

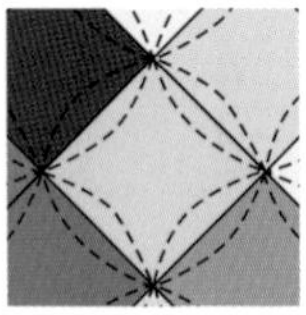

Figure 5

2. Sew a brown mottled button to the center of each A square to finish. ■

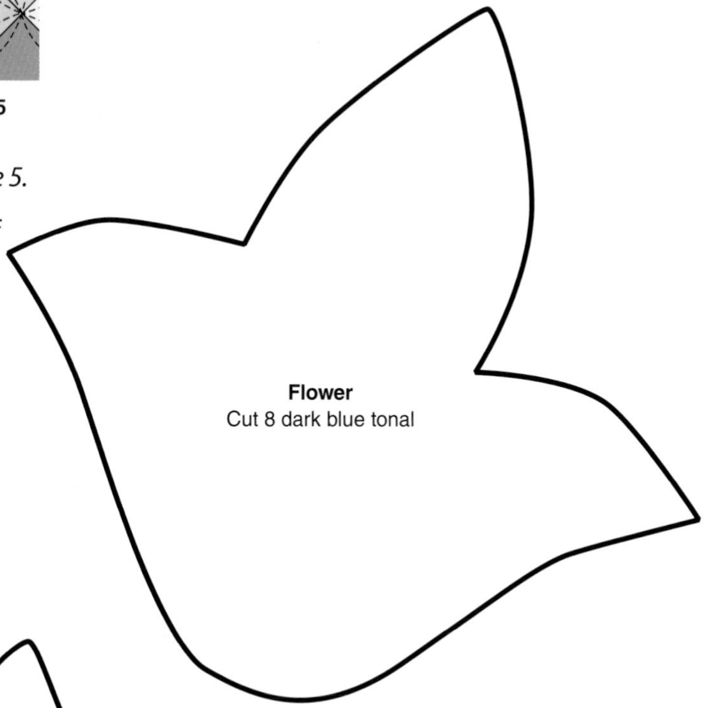

Flower
Cut 8 dark blue tonal

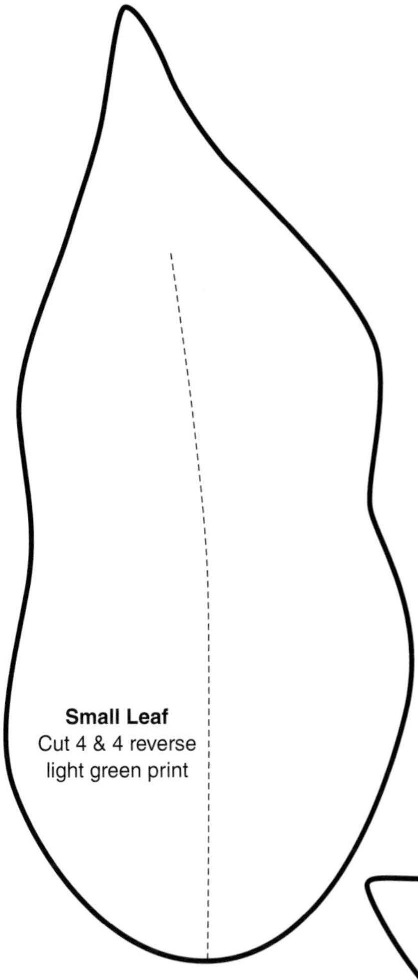

Small Leaf
Cut 4 & 4 reverse
light green print

Large Leaf
Cut 4 tan tonal; reverse & cut 2
light blue & 4 dark green tonals

Black Cats & Spiders

Use precut 5-inch squares in bright autumn colors and add black fabric for the cat and spiders for a fun table runner that will delight the young and the young at heart.

DESIGN BY CHRIS MALONE

PROJECT SPECIFICATIONS

Skill Level: Beginner
Runner Size: 45" x 13½"
Napkin Size: 17" x 17"

MATERIALS

- 30 coordinating Halloween print 5" x 5" squares
- 1 fat quarter black mottled
- 18" x 18" square coordinating plaid for each napkin
- Batting 46" x 14"
- Backing 46" x 14"
- Black and white all-purpose thread
- Quilting thread
- Black and orange embroidery floss
- 2 packages green medium rickrack
- 2 (1") black 2-hole buttons for runner; 1 for each napkin
- 4 (⅝") white 2-hole buttons
- 2 (½") orange 2-hole buttons
- 24" (1½"-wide) sheer black ribbon for each napkin
- ⅝ yard 18"-wide fusible web
- Scrap tear-off fabric stabilizer
- No-fray solution
- Dinner plate or platter
- Basic sewing tools and supplies

Completing the Runner

1. Arrange the 5" x 5" squares in 10 rows of three squares each. **Note:** *Keep in mind where the spider-web embellishment will be, and select lighter fabrics so the stitching lines will show.*

2. Join the squares to make rows; press seams in adjacent rows in opposite directions. Join the rows to complete the pieced center; press seams in one direction.

3. Using a dinner plate or platter as a pattern, round off the corners at one end of the runner. Fold the runner in half crosswise and trim the other end to match as shown in Figure 1.

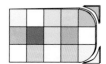

Figure 1

4. Use the trimmed runner to trim the batting and backing to size.

5. Trace the cat appliqué pattern pieces two times each (reversing one tail) onto the paper side of the fusible web, leaving a margin of at least ¼" between shapes. Cut shapes apart, leaving a margin around each one.

6. Iron the paper shapes onto the wrong side of the black tonal; cut out shapes on traced lines. Remove paper backing.

7. Arrange a cat body, tail and head at each end of the runner with the cats' feet 2½" from the bottom edge of the runner; fuse shapes in place with tail first, then body and then head.

8. Using black thread and a machine blanket stitch, stitch around each cat shape to secure in place.

9. Transfer the whiskers pattern to each cat face. Machine-stitch twice on each line with white thread.

10. Referring to the project photo and the Placement Diagram, transfer the spider-leg pattern in the two center squares above each cat.

11. Pin a piece of tear-off stabilizer beneath the marked lines on the wrong side of the runner; machine-stitch on each line twice using black thread; remove stabilizer when stitching is complete.

12. Join one end of each package of rickrack to make one long piece. Press the seam open and apply no-fray solution to the cut ends.

13. Baste rickrack around the edge of the runner with the center of the trim on the ¼" seam allowance as shown in Figure 2; join the ends where the rickrack meets, referring to Figure 3. Trim ends leaving a ¼" seam allowance. Press the seam open and apply no-fray solution to the cut ends.

| Figure 2 | Figure 3 |

14. Place the batting on a flat surface with the backing right side up on top. Place the pieced runner right sides together with the backing; pin to hold flat.

15. Sew all around runner edges, leaving a 5" opening on one straight edge. Trim batting close to seam, clip curves and turn right side out through the opening. Press edges flat.

16. Fold in the seam allowance on the opening; whipstitch opening closed.

17. Topstitch all around very close to the edge.

18. Stitch in the ditch around each cat appliqué.

19. Referring to the photo and the Placement Diagram, transfer the spiderweb pattern to two squares on the runner. Machine-stitch on the lines using black thread.

20. Transfer the curved spider trail pattern to the runner from the outer edge to the spider legs; stitch on the marked lines using black thread.

21. Sew a black button over the center of each set of spider legs using black thread or 3 strands of black embroidery floss, sewing through all layers.

22. Sew two white buttons to each cat face for eyes, using black thread or 3 strands of embroidery floss, sewing through all layers.

23. To finish, sew an orange button to each cat face for a nose using orange thread or 3 strands of orange embroidery floss, sewing through all layers.

Completing the Napkin

1. Fold and press a double ¼" hem along all four sides of a napkin square; stitch to hem.

2. Referring to steps 10 and 11 in Completing the Runner, stitch one set of spider legs on a corner of the napkin.

3. Sew a black button over the center of the spider legs.

4. Fold the napkin and tie with a sheer black ribbon. ■

Napkin
Placement Diagram 17" x 17"

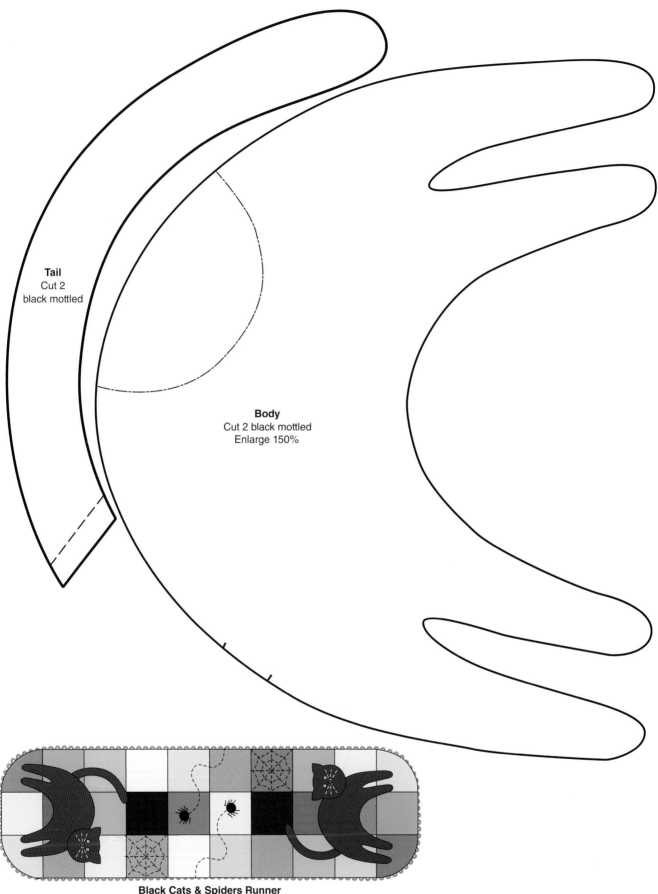

Tail
Cut 2
black mottled

Body
Cut 2 black mottled
Enlarge 150%

Black Cats & Spiders Runner
Placement Diagram 45" x 13½"

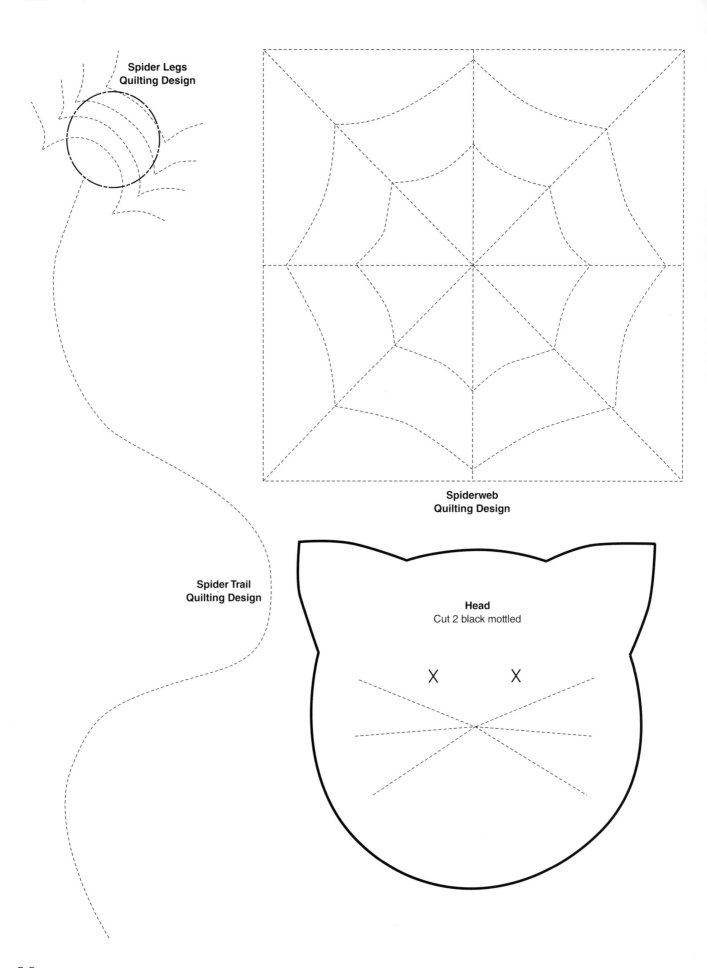

**Spider Legs
Quilting Design**

**Spiderweb
Quilting Design**

**Spider Trail
Quilting Design**

Head
Cut 2 black mottled

Practical
Precuts

Stitch these projects for your own home, and your family and friends will be asking you to make additional ones to match their decor. In this chapter, there are 12 household items—two sets of place mats, three table runners, a bed runner, apron, wall quilt, set of coasters and a three-piece kitchen set. Your home will look better than ever.

Extra X's Bed Runner

Try paper piecing with 2½" strips, using the leftovers for the border. How practical!

DESIGN BY CONNIE RAND

PROJECT SPECIFICATIONS

Skill Level: Intermediate
Runner Size: 60" x 12"
Block Size: 4" x 8"
Number of Blocks: 14

MATERIALS

- 20 light and 10 dark 2½" by fabric width batik strips
- Batting 68" x 20"
- Backing 68" x 20"
- All-purpose thread to match fabrics
- Quilting thread
- Paper for paper piecing
- Basic sewing tools and supplies

Extra X's
4" x 8" Block
Make 14

Cutting

1. Make 29 copies each of the A and B paper-piecing patterns. Cut one copy of each A and B pattern apart to use as templates for cutting fabrics.

2. Cut light and dark batik pieces from the 2½"-wide strips using templates as guides, and adding at least ⅜" around each template for seam allowance.

3. Cut (68) 2½" x 2½" C squares in a variety of colors from remaining 2½"-wide strips.

4. Select four 2½"-wide strips for binding.

Completing the Blocks

1. Pin piece 1 right side up in the No. 1 position on the unmarked side of the paper pattern.

2. Place piece 2 right sides together with piece 1; stitch on the 1–2 line on the marked side of the paper as shown in Figure 1. Press the piece to the right side to cover area 2 and extend ¼" into area 3.

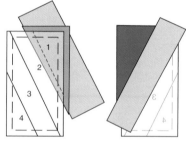

Figure 1

3. Repeat steps 1 and 2 with all pieces in numerical order, referring to the pattern for color placement; press all pieces to the right side after stitching.

4. When stitching is complete, trim outside edges along solid line and remove paper.

5. Repeat to make 28 each A and B units.

6. To complete one Extra X's block, join one A and one B unit to make a row; press seam toward the A unit. Repeat to make two rows.

7. Join the rows referring to the block drawing to complete one block.

8. Repeat steps 6 and 7 to complete a total of 14 blocks.

Completing the Runner Top

1. Join the 14 blocks on the 8" sides to complete the runner center; press seams in one direction.

2. Select and join four C squares to make an end strip as shown in Figure 2; press seams to one side. Repeat to make a second end strip.

Make 2

Make 2

Figure 2

3. Sew an end strip to opposite short ends of the runner center; press seams toward the end strips.

4. Select and join 30 C squares to make a side strip, again referring to Figure 2; press seams to one side. Repeat to make a second side strip.

5. Sew a side strip to opposite long sides of the runner center to complete the runner top; press seams toward the side strips.

Completing the Runner

1. Refer to Finishing Your Quilt on page 176 to sandwich, quilt and bind your runner using the selected 2½"-wide batik strips. ■

Extra X's Bed Runner
Placement Diagram 60" x 12"

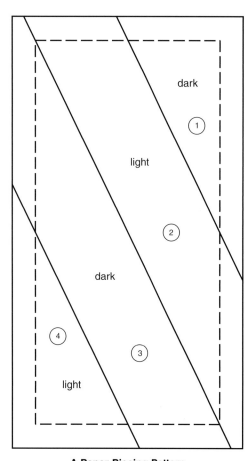

A Paper-Piecing Pattern
Make 29 copies

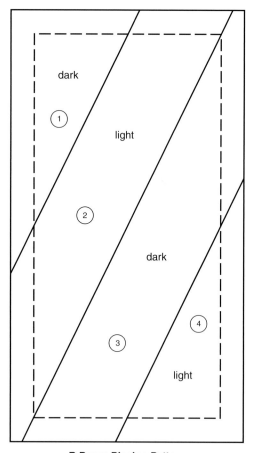

B Paper-Piecing Pattern
Make 29 copies

Chicken Kitchen Table Set

Piece these fun patchwork chickens to decorate your kitchen. A bit of embroidery and buttons add the perfect finishing touches.

DESIGNS BY CHRIS MALONE

PROJECT NOTE

If making all three projects, one fat quarter each of the green, tan, red, gold and rust prints will be sufficient. You will need two fat quarters of the blue print and 1⅝ yards of black floral.

PROJECT SPECIFICATIONS

Skill Level: Intermediate
Runner Size: 42" x 16"
Hot Mat Size: 13" x 13"
Wall Hanging Size: 15" x 15" without tabs
Block Size: 10" x 10"
Number of Blocks: 3 for table runner, and 1 each for hot mat and wall hanging

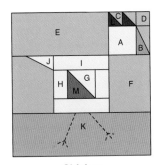

Chicken
10" x 10" Block
Make 3 for table runner, 1 for
hot mat & 1 for wall hanging

Table Runner

MATERIALS

- 1 fat quarter each blue, tan, red and gold tonals
- 1 fat quarter each green and rust prints
- ½ yard black floral
- Batting 50" x 24"
- Backing 50" x 24"
- All-purpose thread to match fabrics
- Quilting thread
- Black embroidery floss
- 3 (⁷⁄₁₆") heat-resistant black buttons
- 9 (⅝") heat-resistant tan buttons
- Water-soluble marker
- Basic sewing tools and supplies

Cutting

1. Cut one 2⅞" x 21" strip tan tonal; subcut strip into two 2⅞" G squares; trim strip to 2½" wide and cut three 2½" A squares.

2. Cut one 4½" x 21" strip tan tonal; subcut strip into six 1½" I rectangles; trim strip to 2½" wide and cut six 1½" H rectangles.

3. Cut one 1⅞" x 21" strip blue tonal; subcut strip into three 1⅞" C squares. Trim strip to 1½" wide and cut three 1½" D squares.

4. Cut one 7½" x 21" strip blue tonal; subcut strip into three 3½" E rectangles.

5. Cut one 4½" x 21" strip blue tonal; subcut strip into six 3½" F rectangles.

6. Prepare templates for B and J using patterns given; cut as directed on patterns.

7. Cut one 1⅞" x 21" strip red tonal; subcut strip into three 1⅞" L squares.

8. Cut seven 2¼" x 21" strips red tonal for binding.

9. Cut one 2⅞" x 21" strip rust print; subcut strip into two 2⅞" M squares.

10. Cut two 3½" x 21" strips green print; subcut strips into three 10½" K rectangles.

11. Cut one 3½" by fabric width strip black floral; subcut strip into four 10½" N strips.

12. Cut two 3½" x 42½" O strips black floral.

Completing the Blocks

1. Draw a diagonal line from corner to corner on the wrong side of each C square. Pin a C square right sides together with an L square; stitch ¼" on each side of the marked line. Cut apart on the marked line referring to Figure 1 to make two C-L units; press seams toward L. Repeat to make six C-L units.

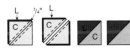

Figure 1

Figure 2

2. Repeat step 1 with G and M to make four G-M units referring to Figure 2; discard one unit.

3. Stitch a gold B to a blue B as shown in Figure 3; press seam toward the gold B. Trim the small extending corners as shown in Figure 4; repeat to make three B-B units.

Figure 3   **Figure 4**

4. To complete one Chicken block, join two C-L units and add D as shown in Figure 5; press seams toward D.

Figure 5   **Figure 6**

5. Sew a B-B unit to an A square and join with the C-L-D unit to complete the head unit as shown in Figure 6; press seam toward A.

6. Sew E to the A edge of the head unit; press seam toward E.

7. Sew H to opposite sides and I to the top and bottom of the G-M unit to complete the body unit as shown in Figure 7; press seams toward H and I pieces.

Figure 7   **Figure 8**

8. Pin a J piece right sides together at the top right corner of one F rectangle; sew along the centerline as shown in Figure 8. Trim seam to ¼", flip J to the right side and press with seam toward F to complete an F-J unit.

9. Sew an F-J unit to the left side and add an F to the opposite side of the body unit as shown in Figure 9.

Figure 9

10. Join the two pieced units and add K to the bottom as shown in Figure 10; press seams toward the head row and K.

Figure 10

11. Transfer feet and legs lines to K under the body section referring to the block drawing and using pattern given.

12. Outline-stitch on the lines using 2 strands black embroidery floss to complete one Chicken block.

13. Repeat steps 4–12 to complete three Chicken blocks.

Completing the Table Runner

1. Transfer the cloud quilting design onto the E area of each block using the pattern given and a water-soluble marker.

2. Join the three Chicken blocks with four N strips beginning and ending with N; press seams toward strips.

3. Sew an O strip to opposite long sides of the pieced center to complete the pieced top; press seams toward O strips.

4. Sandwich batting between the pieced top and prepared backing; pin or baste layers together to hold flat.

5. Quilt on marked lines and in the ditch of seams around chicken pieces and between blocks and N and O strips and as desired by hand or machine. Trim batting and backing even with the top edges.

6. Join the binding strips on short ends with diagonal seams to make one long strip; trim seams to ¼" and press open.

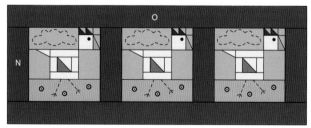

Chicken Table Runner
Placement Diagram 42" x 16"

7. Fold binding strip in half with wrong sides together along length; press. Apply to pieced top runner edges, mitering corners and overlapping ends; turn to the back side and hand-stitch in place.

8. Sew a black button ⅝" in from the top and side edges of A in each head unit for eye as shown in Figure 11.

Figure 11

9. Sew three tan buttons randomly to the K ground section of each block to finish the runner.

Chicken Hot Mat

MATERIALS

- 1 fat quarter each blue, tan, red and gold tonals
- 1 fat quarter each green and rust prints
- 1 fat quarter black floral
- Insulated batting 13½" x 13½"
- Cotton batting 13½" x 13½"
- Backing 13½" x 13½"
- All-purpose thread to match fabrics
- Quilting thread
- Black embroidery floss
- 1 (⁷⁄₁₆") black heat-resistant button
- 3 (⅝") tan heat-resistant buttons
- Water-soluble marker
- Basic sewing tools and supplies

Cutting

1. Cut one 2⅞" x 21" strip tan tonal; subcut strip into one 2⅞" G square; trim strip to 2½" wide and cut one 2½" A square.

2. Cut one 1½" x 21" strip tan tonal; subcut strip into two 2½" H rectangles and two 4½" I rectangles.

3. Cut one 1⅞" x 21" strip blue tonal; subcut strip into one 1⅞" C square. Trim strip to 1½" and cut one 1½" D square.

4. Cut one 3½" x 21" strip blue tonal; subcut strip into one 7½" E rectangle and two 4½" F rectangles.

5. Prepare templates for B and J using patterns given; cut as directed on each piece.

6. Cut one 1⅞" x 21" strip red tonal; subcut strip into one 1⅞" L square.

7. Cut one 2⅞" x 21" strip rust print; subcut strip into one 2⅞" M square.

8. Cut one 3½" x 21" strip green print; subcut strip into one 10½" K rectangle.

9. Cut one 2" x 21" strip black floral; subcut strip into two 10½" P strips.

10. Cut two 2" x 13½" Q strips black floral.

Completing the Block

1. Refer to steps 1–12 for Completing the Blocks for the table runner except make two C-L units and one each B-B, F-J and G-M units to complete one Chicken block.

Completing the Hot Mat

1. Sew P strips to opposite sides and Q strips to the top and bottom of the Chicken block; press seams toward P and Q strips.

2. Transfer the cloud quilting design onto the E area of the block using the pattern given and a water-soluble marker.

3. Lay the cotton batting square on a flat surface and place the insulated batting on top; place the backing square right side up on the batting layers and pin the Chicken block right side down on the backing/batting layers.

4. Sew all around, leaving a 5" opening on one side; trim batting layers close to seam and clip corners.

5. Turn right side out through opening; press edges and corners flat. Turn in opening edges ¼"; press. Hand-stitch opening closed.

6. Quilt on marked lines and in the ditch of seams around chicken pieces, and between the block and the Q and P strips, and as desired by hand or machine.

7. Sew a black button ⅝" in from the top and side edges of A in the head unit for eye, again referring to Figure 11.

8. Sew three tan buttons randomly to the K ground section of the block to finish the hot mat.

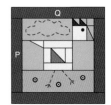

Chicken Hot Mat
Placement Diagram 13" x 13"

Chicken Wall Hanging

MATERIALS

- 1 fat quarter each blue, tan, red and gold tonals
- 1 fat quarter each green and rust prints
- 1 fat quarter black floral
- Batting 15½" x 15½" and scraps for tabs
- Backing 15½" x 15½"
- All-purpose thread to match fabrics
- Quilting thread
- Black embroidery floss
- 1 (⁷⁄₁₆") black button
- 3 (⅝") tan buttons
- 5 (¾") cover button kits
- 2 (1") plastic rings
- Water-soluble marker
- Basic sewing tools and supplies

Cutting

1. Cut one 2⅞" x 21" strip tan tonal; subcut strip into one 2⅞" G square; trim strip to 2½" wide and cut one 2½" A square.

2. Cut one 1½" x 21" strip tan tonal; subcut strip into two 2½" H rectangles and two 4½" I rectangles.

3. Cut one 1⅞" x 21" strip blue tonal; subcut strip into one 1⅞" C square. Trim strip to 1½" and cut one 1½" D square.

4. Cut one 3½" x 21" strip blue tonal; subcut strip into one 7½" E rectangle and two 4½" F rectangles.

5. Prepare templates for B, J and the hanging tab using patterns given; cut B and J pieces as directed on each piece.

6. Cut two 1½"-diameter circles gold tonal for cover buttons.

7. Cut one 1⅞" x 21" strip red tonal; subcut strip into one 1⅞" L square and three 1½"-diameter circles for cover buttons.

8. Cut one 2⅞" x 21" strip rust print; subcut strip into one 2⅞" M square.

9. Cut one 3½" x 21" strip green print; subcut strip into one 10½" K rectangle.

10. Cut one 3" x 21" strip black floral; subcut strip into two 10½" R strips.

11. Cut two 3" x 15½" S strips black floral.

Completing the Block

1. Refer to steps 1–12 for Completing the Blocks for the table runner except make two C-L units and one each B-B, F-J and G-M units to complete one Chicken block.

Completing the Wall Quilt

1. Sew R strips to opposite sides and S strips to the top and bottom of the Chicken block; press seams toward R and S strips.

2. Transfer the cloud quilting design onto the E area of the block using the pattern given and a water-soluble marker.

3. Trace the hanging tab pattern five times onto the wrong side of the rust print, leaving ½" between each shape. Fold the fabric in half with right sides together and the traced shapes on top; pin to a scrap of batting.

4. Stitch around each tab piece on the marked lines, leaving the straight end open. Cut out each tab ¼" from the seam; trim batting close to stitching and clip curves.

5. Turn the tabs right side out through the open ends and press edges flat. Topstitch ¼" around curved edges to complete the tabs.

6. Evenly space and baste the tabs along the bottom edge of the bordered Chicken block with the edge of the first and last tab ⅜" in from the edge of the bordered block as shown in Figure 12.

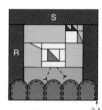

Figure 12 ⅜"

7. Lay the batting square on a flat surface; place the backing square right side up on the batting layers and pin the Chicken block right side down on the backing/batting layers, making sure the tabs are tucked between the Chicken block and the backing square.

8. Sew all around, leaving a 5" opening on one side; trim batting layers close to seam and clip corners.

9. Turn right side out through opening; press edges and corners flat. Turn in opening edges ¼"; press. Hand-stitch opening closed.

10. Quilt on marked lines, in the ditch of seams around chicken piecing, ¼" from the seams on both edges of each R and S strip, and as desired by hand or machine.

11. Sew a black button ⅝" in from the top and side edges of the A in the head unit for eye, again referring to Figure 11.

12. Sew three tan buttons randomly to the K ground section of the block.

13. Follow manufacturer's instructions to complete two gold and three red cover buttons;

center and sew buttons ½" from the bottom edge of each hanging tab.

14. Sew a plastic ring to the top back corners to finish the wall hanging. ■

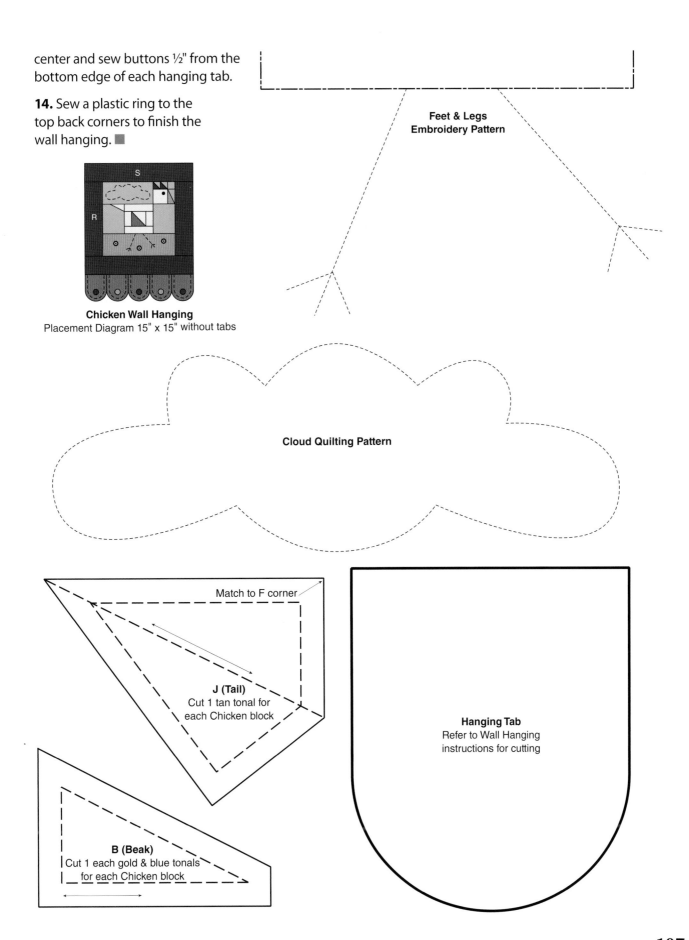

Chicken Wall Hanging
Placement Diagram 15" x 15" without tabs

**Feet & Legs
Embroidery Pattern**

Cloud Quilting Pattern

Match to F corner

J (Tail)
Cut 1 tan tonal for
each Chicken block

B (Beak)
Cut 1 each gold & blue tonals
for each Chicken block

Hanging Tab
Refer to Wall Hanging
instructions for cutting

Charmed Runner & Coasters

Using a charm pack is a very economical and fun way to make a very scrappy, but still color-coordinated, project. Make the coasters from the charm squares left over from the runner.

DESIGNS BY CHRIS MALONE

Runner

PROJECT SPECIFICATIONS

Skill Level: Beginner
Runner Size: 51" x 12¾"

MATERIALS

- 22 total coordinating 5" x 5" print A squares
- 2 each rose and yellow 5" x 5" print squares
- 4 (5" x 5") green squares
- ⅓ yard brown solid
- ½ yard brown print
- Backing 59" x 20"
- Batting 59" x 20"
- All-purpose thread to match fabrics
- Quilting thread
- Pink and yellow size 8 pearl cotton
- ½ yard lightweight nonwoven interfacing
- ¼"-wide bias pressing bar
- Basic sewing tools and supplies

Cutting

1. Cut 1⅛"-wide bias strips from brown solid to total 45" when seamed for stems.

2. Cut 2¼"-wide bias strips from brown print to total 170" when seamed for binding.

Completing the Runner

1. Arrange and join the A squares into six inside rows with three A squares each, and two end rows with two A squares each referring to Figure 1. Press seams in adjacent rows in opposite directions.

Figure 1

2. Join the stitched rows in staggered rows as arranged to complete the pieced background; press seams in one direction.

Completing the Appliqué

1. Prepare templates using patterns given.

2. Draw a total of 16 leaf shapes onto the wrong side of the 5" x 5" green squares, leaving a margin of at least ¼" between the shapes.

3. Pin each traced square traced side up onto the lightweight, nonwoven interfacing; stitch all around each traced leaf on drawn lines. Cut out each shape ⅛" from the stitching line; clip curves and tips as shown in Figure 2.

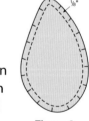

Figure 2

4. Cut a slash through the interfacing side only, referring to pattern for positioning; turn each leaf right side out through the slashed opening. Press edges flat.

5. Prepare the five rose and four yellow flower shapes using the 5" x 5" rose and yellow print squares referring to steps 2–4. Repeat with flower centers using leftover pieces from flowers, cutting 5 yellow and 4 rose centers.

6. Fold the brown bias vine strip in half with wrong sides together along length; stitch a scant ¼" seam down the length. Trim seam to ⅛"; insert the bias pressing bar and press seam open with seam running down the center of the length as shown in Figure 3.

Figure 3

7. Referring to the Placement Diagram and project photo, arrange the vine in gentle curves down the length of the table runner, beginning and ending the vine about 4" from the corners of the ends of the runner; baste or pin and hand-stitch in place.

8. Pin a center to each flower; hand-stitch in place. **Note:** *When appliquéing using this interfacing method, stitch through the edge of the fabric, not the interfacing.*

9. Arrange and hand-stitch the nine flowers along the vine with a rose flower at the center and at each end of the vine and the remaining flowers alternating and evenly spaced in between. Arrange and hand-stitch the leaves in place referring to the Placement Diagram for positioning.

10. Using 1 strand of pearl cotton, make three French knots in the center of each flower, using pink for the rose flowers and yellow for the yellow flowers.

Completing the Runner

1. Sandwich the batting between the completed top and the prepared backing; pin or baste together to hold.

2. Quilt as desired by hand or machine; remove pins or basting. Trim excess backing and batting even with the edge of the runner top. **Note:** *The sample was machine-quilted, stitching in the ditch around each appliqué shape. In addition, the leaf pattern was used to stitch a stem and leaf shape in the open squares as shown in Figure 4.*

Figure 4

3. Join the bias binding strips on the short ends with diagonal seams to make one long strip as shown in Figure 5. Trim seams to ¼" and press

open. Fold the strip in half with wrong sides together along length; press carefully to avoid stretching.

Figure 5

4. Refer to page 176 for binding instructions. When approaching an inside corner, pin the binding miter to the right side, and then mirror the miter on the back side and stitch in place, adding a few stitches to the miter fold on the front and back as shown in Figure 6.

Figure 6

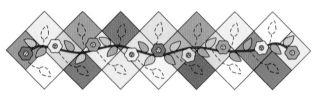

Charmed Runner
Placement Diagram 51" x 12¾"

Charmed Coasters

PROJECT SPECIFICATIONS

Skill Level: Beginner
Coaster Size: 4½" x 4½"
Number of Coasters: 4

MATERIALS

- 8 coordinating 5" x 5" print squares for coaster fronts and backs
- 1 (5" x 5") square each rose, yellow and green fabrics or scraps
- 1 fat quarter brown solid
- ⅓ yard brown print
- 4 squares batting 6" x 6"
- All-purpose thread to match fabrics
- Quilting thread
- Pink and yellow size 8 pearl cotton
- ¼ yard lightweight nonwoven interfacing
- ¼"-wide bias pressing bar
- Basic sewing tools and supplies

Cutting

1. Cut four 1⅛" x 6" bias strips brown solid for stems.

2. Cut three 2¼" by fabric width strips brown print for binding.

Completing the Appliqué

1. Prepare appliqué templates using patterns given.

2. Draw four leaf shapes onto the wrong side of the 5" x 5" green square, leaving a margin of at least ¼" between the shapes. ***Note:*** *For variety, more than one square of green print may be used.*

3. Pin each traced square traced side up onto the lightweight, nonwoven interfacing; stitch all around each traced leaf on drawn lines. Cut out each shape ⅛" from the stitching line; clip curves and tips as shown in Figure 2.

4. Cut a slash through the interfacing side only, referring to pattern for positioning; turn each leaf right side out through the slashed opening. Press edges flat.

5. Prepare the two each rose and yellow flower shapes in the same manner using the 5" x 5" rose and yellow print squares. Repeat with flower centers using leftover pieces from flowers.

6. Fold each brown bias vine strip in half with wrong sides together along length; stitch a scant ¼" seam down the length. Trim seam to ⅛"; insert the bias pressing bar and press seam open with seam running down the center of the length as shown in Figure 3.

7. Select one of the coordinating 5" x 5" squares for coaster front; mark a point 3" up from the bottom right corner and another point 4" to the left of the corner as shown in Figure 7.

Figure 7

8. Pin the ends of one vine piece at these points and curve the center section into a gentle arc as shown in Figure 8; pin to hold. Hand-stitch the vine piece in place.

Figure 8

9. Arrange and hand-stitch a leaf and then a flower shape along the vine referring to the Placement Diagram for positioning of pieces. ***Note:*** *When appliquéing using this interfacing method, stitch through the edge of the fabric, not the interfacing.*

10. Using 1 strand of pearl cotton, make three French knots in the center of each flower, using pink for the rose flowers and yellow for the yellow flowers.

Completing the Coasters

1. Sandwich a 6" x 6" batting square between the completed top and a 5" x 5" backing square; pin or baste together to hold.

2. Quilt as desired by hand or machine; remove pins or basting. Trim excess backing and batting even with the edges of the coaster top. ***Note:*** *The sample was machine-quilted, stitching in the ditch around each appliqué shape.*

3. Join the binding strips on the short ends with diagonal seams to make one long strip as shown in Figure 5. Trim seams to ¼" and press open. Fold the strip in half with wrong sides together along length; press.

4. Bind edges referring to page 176. ■

Charmed Coaster
Placement Diagram 4½" x 4½"

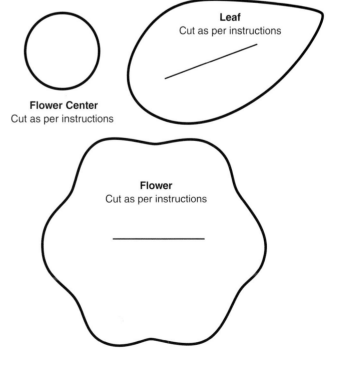

Flower Center
Cut as per instructions

Leaf
Cut as per instructions

Flower
Cut as per instructions

Fern Place Mats

Use batiks to create lovely place mats. Precut strips that are 1½ inches wide make them extra quick and easy to complete.

DESIGN BY CONNIE KAUFFMAN

PROJECT SPECIFICATIONS

Skill Level: Beginner
Place Mat Size: 17½" x 13"

MATERIALS

Makes 2 place mats
- 30 coordinating 1½" by fabric width batik strips
- 1 fat quarter dark green batik
- ½ yard coordinating backing fabric
- ½ yard coordinating batik for binding
- 2 rectangles batting 20" x 15"
- Neutral-color all-purpose thread
- Quilting thread
- Invisible thread
- 2 (9" x 12") sheets paper-backed fusible web
- Basic sewing tools and supplies

Cutting

1. Select one light-color 1½"-wide strip for center; cut one 6" strip for piece 1.

2. Cut two 20" x 15" backing rectangles from the coordinating backing fabric.

3. Cut four 2¼" by fabric width strips from the binding fabric.

Completing the Place Mat Tops

1. Select a second 1½"-wide strip and sew to one side of one 6" piece 1 strip; trim strip even with piece 1 as shown in Figure 1; press seam toward added strip.

Figure 1

2. Repeat with the same strip on the opposite long side of piece 1 to complete the center unit as shown in Figure 2.

Figure 2

3. Select another strip; sew to each short end of the center unit, trim and press seams toward added strips as shown in Figure 3.

 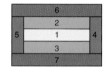

Figure 3   **Figure 4**

4. Select another strip and add to the pieced unit as in step 3 and as shown in Figure 4.

5. Continue adding strips in numerical order referring to Figure 5, trimming and pressing as you sew, to complete one place mat top. Repeat to make a second top.

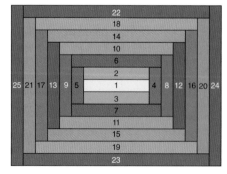

Figure 5

Completing the Appliqué

1. Trace a fern shape onto the paper backing of each fusible-web sheet using the pattern given.

2. Cut out shapes, leaving a margin around each one.

3. Fuse the shapes to the wrong side of the dark green batik; cut out shapes on traced lines. Remove the paper backing from each shape.

4. Arrange and fuse a fern shape onto each of the place mat tops referring to the Placement Diagram for positioning.

5. Using invisible thread, stitch close to the edge of each fern shape to secure.

Completing the Place Mats

1. Refer to Finishing Your Quilt on page 176 to sandwich, quilt and bind each place mat to finish. ◼

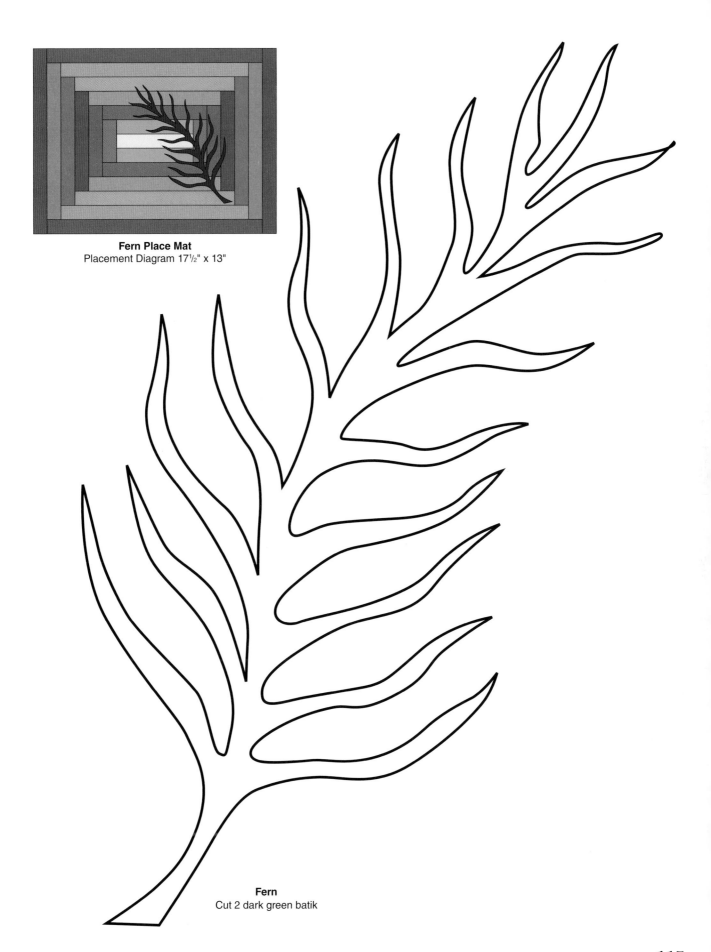

Fern Place Mat
Placement Diagram 17½" x 13"

Fern
Cut 2 dark green batik

Lollipop Spring

This whimsical quilt has lots of color and pizzazz. Depending on your choice of fabric for the appliqué pieces, the flowers will either pop off the table runner or nestle in a bed of spring florals.

DESIGN BY WENDY SHEPPARD

PROJECT SPECIFICATIONS

Skill Level: Beginner
Runner Size: 38" x 18"
Block Size: 10" x 10"
Number of Blocks: 3

MATERIALS

- 19 coordinating 2½" by fabric width strips including pink, white, blue, brown, green and red prints and tonal dots
- 10" x 10" squares: 3 red tonal dots, 1 white/red dots and 4 green tonal dots
- Backing 42" x 22"
- Batting 42" x 22"
- Cream all-purpose thread
- 2 each ⅜" and ⅝" ladybug buttons
- 4 (9" x 12") sheets paper-backed fusible web
- 1 yard ¼"-wide fusible web
- ⅜" bias pressing bar
- Basic sewing tools and supplies

Cutting

Note: Both the 2½"-wide precut strips and the 10" x 10" precut squares are from the same fabric collection. There are usually 40 precut strips per package, giving plenty of choices to use for this runner. Or make a second runner for a friend.

1. Cut nine 2½" A squares from one 2½"-wide blue print strip.

2. Cut (12) 2½" B squares from one 2½"-wide pink print strip.

3. Cut six 2½" C squares and six 4½" E rectangles from one 2½"-wide white print strip.

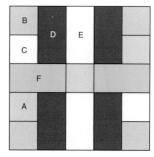

Lollipop Spring
10" x 10" Block
Make 3

4. Cut (12) 4½" D rectangles from two 2½"-wide red print strips.

5. Cut six 4½" F rectangles from one 2½"-wide green print strip.

6. Select five white print and tonal dots 2½"-wide strips and trim to 1½" wide; subcut the trimmed strips into two 10½" G, two 32½" H and two 34½" J strips.

7. Select one brown tonal dots 2½"-wide strip and trim to 1½" wide; subcut the trimmed strip into two 12½" I strips.

8. Select three brown tonal dots 2½"-wide strips; subcut strips into two 34½" K strips and two 18½" L strips.

9. Select three 2½"-wide green strips for binding.

10. Trace flower and leaf shapes onto the paper side of the fusible web leaving ½" between pieces and referring to patterns for number to cut; cut out shapes, leaving a margin around each one.

11. Fuse shapes to the wrong side of the 10" x 10" squares as directed on pieces for color; cut out shapes on traced lines. Remove paper backing.

12. Select one 2½"-wide strip green tonal dots for stems.

Completing the Lollipop Blocks

1. Sew A to B; press seam toward A. Repeat to make two A-B units.

2. Sew D to each A-B unit to make two A-B-D units as shown in Figure 1; press seams toward D.

3. Repeat steps 1 and 2 to make two B-C-D units, again referring to Figure 1.

Figure 1

4. Join one each A-B-D and B-C-D units with E to make an E row as shown in Figure 2; press seams toward D. Repeat to make a second E row.

Figure 2

5. Sew A between two F pieces to make an A-F row as shown in Figure 3; press seams toward A.

Figure 3

6. Sew the A-F row between the two E rows to complete one Lollipop Spring block as shown in Figure 4; press seams toward the A-F row.

Figure 4

7. Repeat steps 1–6 to complete a total of three Lollipop Spring blocks.

Completing the Runner Top

1. Arrange and join the three blocks as shown in Figure 5; press seams in one direction.

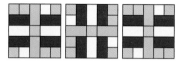

Figure 5

2. Sew the G strips to opposite short ends and H strips to opposite long sides of the block center; press seams toward G and H strips.

3. Sew the I strips to opposite short ends and J strips to opposite long sides of the block center; press seams toward I and J strips.

4. Sew a K strip to opposite long sides and L strips to the short ends to complete the pieced top; press seams toward K and L strips.

Completing the Appliqué

1. Trim the selected stem strip to 1½" wide; fold the strip with wrong sides together along length. Stitch raw edges together using a ¼" seam allowance.

2. After stitching, insert the ⅜" bias bar and center and press seam open to complete the stem strip as shown in Figure 6.

Figure 6

3. Cut the stem strip into two 5¼" and two 6¾" lengths.

4. Apply ¼" fusible web to the wrong side of each stem piece, referring to the manufacturer's instructions.

5. Arrange and fuse one long stem, five large leaves and one large flower motif on the border area of one end of the pieced runner top, referring to the Placement Diagram for positioning of pieces.

6. Repeat with one short stem, six small leaves and one medium flower motif next to the large flower.

7. Repeat steps 5 and 6 on the opposite end of the pieced runner top, again referring to the Placement Diagram for positioning.

8. Using cream thread and a medium-size blanket stitch, sew all around each piece to secure.

Completing the Runner

1. Refer to Finishing Your Quilt on page 176 to sandwich, quilt and bind your runner.

2. Sew a ⅜" ladybug button to one small leaf on each small flower motif and a ⅝" ladybug button to one large leaf on each large flower motif to finish. ■

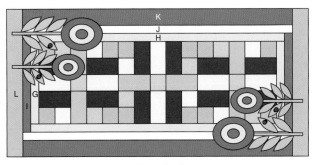

Lollipop Spring
Placement Diagram 38" x 18"

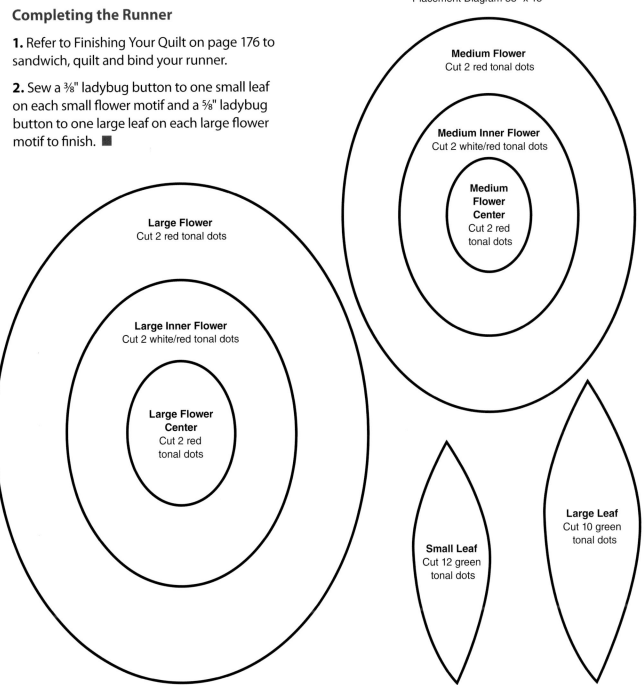

Medium Flower
Cut 2 red tonal dots

Medium Inner Flower
Cut 2 white/red tonal dots

Medium Flower Center
Cut 2 red tonal dots

Large Flower
Cut 2 red tonal dots

Large Inner Flower
Cut 2 white/red tonal dots

Large Flower Center
Cut 2 red tonal dots

Small Leaf
Cut 12 green tonal dots

Large Leaf
Cut 10 green tonal dots

With a Twist of Orange

Using charm squares and yardage, create a wall quilt that will brighten your kitchen. Every meal will be a time to celebrate.

DESIGN BY JULIE HIGGINS

Wall Quilt

PROJECT SPECIFICATIONS

Skill Level: Intermediate
Wall Quilt Size: 45" x 33"
Block Size: 6" x 6"
Number of Blocks: 24

MATERIALS

- 24 coordinating 5" x 5" A squares
- ⅛ yard orange mottled
- ⅛ yard yellow mottled
- ⅛ yard lime green tonal
- ⅛ yard orange check
- ⅝ yard orange print
- 1 yard bright blue mottled
- Batting 53" x 41"
- Backing 53" x 41"
- Neutral-color all-purpose thread
- Basic sewing tools and supplies

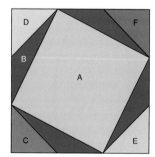

Twist
6" x 6" Block
Make 24 for quilt &
6 for each place mat

Cutting

1. Prepare a template for B using pattern given; cut 96 from bright blue mottled. ***Note:*** *All pieces must be cut on the fabric the same way—there are no reverse or mirror-image shapes. Place template right side up on the right side of the fabric when cutting all pieces.*

2. Cut two 1½" x 36½" G strips and two 1½" x 26½" H strips bright blue blue mottled.

3. Cut one 2⅞" by fabric width strip each orange mottled (C), yellow mottled (D), lime green tonal (E) and orange check (F); subcut each strip into (12) 2⅞" squares. Cut each square in half on one diagonal to make 24 each C, D, E and F triangles.

4. Cut two 4" x 38½" I strips and two 4" x 33½" J strips orange print.

Completing the Blocks

1. Sew a B piece to each side of an A square; press seams toward B. ***Note:*** *Be careful to match the ends of the seam allowances at the corners very carefully as shown in Figure 1.*

Figure 1

2. Sew one each C, D, E and F triangle to each A-B unit to complete the 24 identical Twist blocks, placing the triangles in the same position on each block; press seams toward the triangles.

Completing the Top

1. Arrange and join six Twist blocks to make a row, orienting the triangles in the same position in the row as shown in Figure 2; press seams in one direction. Repeat to make four rows.

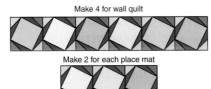

Make 4 for wall quilt

Make 2 for each place mat

Figure 2

2. Join the rows, alternating seam pressing from row to row, to complete the pieced center; press seams in one direction.

3. Sew a G strip to opposite long sides and H strips to the short ends of the pieced center; press seams toward G and H strips.

4. Sew an I strip to opposite long sides and J strips to the short ends of the pieced center; press seams toward I and J strips.

Completing the Quilt

1. Fold the completed top horizontally and vertically, and crease to mark the side and end centers.

2. To mark scallop placement, measure and mark a point at the center crease on the wrong side of the I strip 3¾" from seam as shown in Figure 3. Measure 1½" on one side of the crease and mark a point at the seam line; measure up 2⅜" from that point and mark to make the first dip in the scallop, again referring to Figure 3.

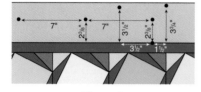

Figure 3

3. Measure and mark 7" from last marked inside point for the center of the next dip in the scallop, again referring to Figure 3. Measure and mark a point 3½" from the 2⅜" point and 3½" from the seam to mark the center of the scallop curve, referring to Figure 3. Repeat with a second 7" and 3½" measurement. Measure out 2⅜" and mark points for the scallop dips.

4. Repeat step 3 on the opposite side of the center mark.

5. Draw center peak from the 3¾" center point to the 2⅜" points on either side, referring to Figure 4. Using a circular object, such as a plate, draw scallop shapes on the marked border strips as shown in Figure 4.

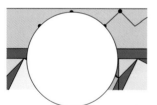

Figure 4

6. Measure and mark a point at the center crease of strip J 2⅜" and mark a point; measure and mark a point 7" on each side of the center for the scallop dips as shown in Figure 5. Repeat step 5 to mark scallop shapes on each end of the pieced center, and connecting corners, again referring to Figure 5.

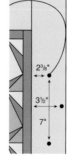

Figure 5

7. Place the batting on a flat surface with the backing piece right side up on top; place the completed top right sides together with the backing. Stitch on the marked scallop line all around, leaving a 4" opening on one side. Trim excess to leave a ¼" seam allowance all around and clip into dips as shown in Figure 6.

Figure 6

8. Turn right side out through the opening; press edges flat. Turn opening edges in ¼" and hand-stitch close; press.

9. Quilt as desired by hand or machine to finish.

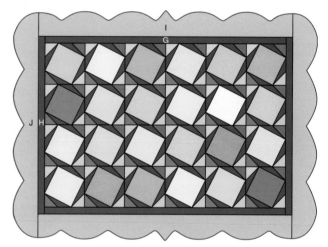

With a Twist of Orange Wall Quilt
Placement Diagram 45" x 33"

Place Mats

PROJECT SPECIFICATIONS

Skill Level: Intermediate
Place Mat Size: 27" x 21"
Block Size: 6" x 6"
Number of Blocks: 6 per place mat (12)

MATERIALS

- 12 coordinating 5" x 5" A squares
- ⅛ yard orange mottled
- ⅛ yard yellow mottled
- ⅛ yard lime green tonal
- ⅛ yard orange check
- ⅜ yard orange print
- ½ yard bright blue mottled
- 2 batting rectangles 31" x 25"

- 2 backing rectangles 31" x 25"
- Neutral-color all-purpose thread
- Quilting thread
- Basic sewing tools and supplies

Cutting

1. Prepare a template for B using pattern given; cut 48 from bright blue mottled. **Note:** *All pieces must be cut on the fabric the same way—there are no reverse or mirror-image shapes. Place template right side up when cutting all pieces.*

2. Cut two 1½" by fabric width strips bright blue mottled; subcut strips into two 18½" K strips and two 14½" L strips.

3. Cut one 2⅞" by fabric width strip each orange mottled (C), yellow mottled (D), lime green tonal (E) and orange check (F); subcut each strip into six 2⅞" squares. Cut each square in half on one diagonal to make 12 each C, D, E and F triangles.

4. Cut two 4" by fabric width strips orange print; subcut strips into two 20½" M strips and two 22½" N strips.

Completing the Blocks

1. Sew a B piece to each side of an A square; press seams toward B. **Note:** *Be careful to match the ends of the seam allowances at the corners very carefully as shown in Figure 1.*

2. Sew one each C, D, E and F triangle to each A-B unit to complete the 24 identical Twist blocks, placing the triangles in the same position on each block; press seams toward the triangles.

Completing the Tops

1. To complete one place mat top, arrange and join three Twist blocks to make a row, orienting the triangles in the same position in the row, again referring to Figure 2; press seams in one direction. Repeat to make two rows.

2. Join the rows, alternating seam pressing from row to row, to complete the pieced center; press seams in one direction.

3. Sew a K strip to opposite long sides and L strips to the short ends of the pieced center; press seams toward K and L strips.

4. Sew an M strip to opposite long sides and N strips to the short ends of the pieced center; press seams toward M and N strips.

Completing the Place Mats

1. Refer to Completing the Quilt steps 1–6 and Figure 7 to mark two scallops on each end, and one full and two partial scallops on each side of each place mat top, eliminating the center peaks.

2. Place one batting rectangle on a flat surface with one backing piece right side up on top; place a completed top right sides together with the backing. Stitch on the marked scallop line all around, leaving a 4" opening on one side. Trim excess to leave a ¼" seam allowance all around and clip into dips, again referring to Figure 6.

Figure 7

3. Turn right side out through the opening; press edges flat. Turn opening edges in ¼" and hand-stitch close; press.

4. Quilt as desired by hand or machine to finish.

5. Repeat steps 1–4 to complete the second place mat. ■

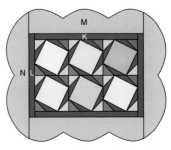

With a Twist of Orange Place Mat
Placement Diagram 27" x 21"

B
Cut 96 bright blue mottled for quilt
Cut 24 bright blue mottled for each place mat

Note: *Place template right side up on the right side of the fabric when tracing/cutting*

Spring Butterflies Apron

The sashiko-stitched pocket and butterfly design give this practical apron an extra-special look. How-to instructions for sashiko stitching are included.

DESIGN BY SUSAN FLETCHER FROM ALDERSPRING DESIGN

PROJECT SPECIFICATIONS

Skill Level: Beginner
Apron Size: 20" x 22" excluding ties

MATERIALS

- 20 coordinating 1½" by fabric width strips
- ⅝ yard coordinating solid for pocket, pocket lining and waistband
- ¾ yard coordinating print for apron backing
- All-purpose thread to match fabrics
- 10" x 13" rectangle white lightweight fusible nonwoven interfacing
- White and blue No. 5 pearl cotton
- Long, hand-stitching needle with a large eye
- Basic sewing tools and supplies

Cutting

1. Cut each 1½" by fabric width strip to 22¾" long for A.

2. Cut two 4" by fabric width B strips coordinating solid.

3. Cut one 10" by fabric width strip coordinating solid; subcut strip into two 13" C rectangles for pocket and pocket lining.

4. Cut one backing piece 20½" x 22¾".

Stitching the Sashiko Pocket

1. Lay one 10" x 13" interfacing rectangle over the sashiko butterfly design with glue side down; trace the design onto the interfacing.

2. Lift the interfacing and fuse it to the wrong side of the C pocket rectangle.

3. Cut a comfortable length of white No. 5 pearl cotton and knot at one end. Insert the needle into the wrong side of the fabric, then about ⅜" along the stitching line push the needle back through to the right side of the fabric.

4. Continue stitching in this manner until you near the end of the thread. Pass the needle under a few stitches on the wrong side of the fabric to secure. For subsequent threads, begin by passing the needle under 2 or 3 stitches on the wrong side of the fabric.

5. When all white stitching is complete, repeat with the blue pearl cotton to stitch the butterfly designs.

6. When all stitching is complete, press carefully.

7. Lay the stitched pocket right sides together on the pocket lining; stitch all around, leaving a 4" opening on one side. Clip corners; turn right side out through the opening.

8. Press edges flat. Press ¼" to the inside on each edge of the opening; hand-stitch opening closed to finish the pocket.

Completing the Apron

1. Join the A strips with right sides together along length to make the pieced apron panel; press seams in one direction.

2. Trim the stitched apron panel to 20½" x 22¾", if necessary. Fold and place a pin to mark the center of the top 20½" edge of the panel.

3. Center and stitch the completed pocket 4" up from the bottom edge, topstitching the sides and bottom to complete the apron. **Note:** *Be careful to align the pocket parallel to a seam joining the A strips.*

4. Lay the apron front on the backing piece right sides together; stitch around sides and across the bottom. Trim corners; turn right side out. Press edges flat.

5. Cut one B strip in half to make two 4" x 21" strips; sew one of these strips to each end of the remaining B strip to make the waistband/tie strip.

6. Fold the strip in half along the length with wrong sides together and press to form a crease; unfold. Press short ends and one long edge ½" to the wrong side referring to Figure 1.

Figure 1

7. Fold the waistband/tie strip in half and place a pin to mark the center on the unpressed edge as shown in Figure 2.

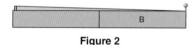

Figure 2

8. With right sides together, center the waistband/tie strip with unpressed raw edge along the top 20½" raw edge of the apron panel as shown in Figure 3; pin to hold.

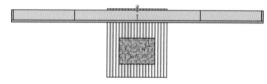

Figure 3

9. Stitch the waistband/tie strip to the apron panel using a ½" seam allowance as shown in Figure 4.

Figure 6

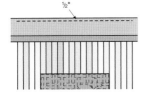

Figure 4

10. Press the stitched waistband/tie strip up. Fold the strip along the previously pressed lengthwise center fold, enclosing stitched edges as shown in Figure 5. Continue matching edges of strip as it extends beyond the panel to make ties; topstitch ⅛" from the folded edge/edges carefully all around as shown in Figure 6 to complete the apron.

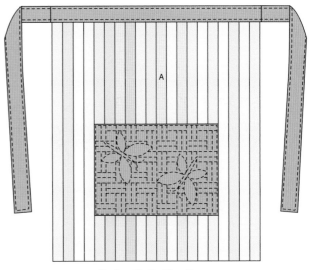

Spring Butterflies Apron
Placement Diagram 20" x 22" excluding ties

Figure 5

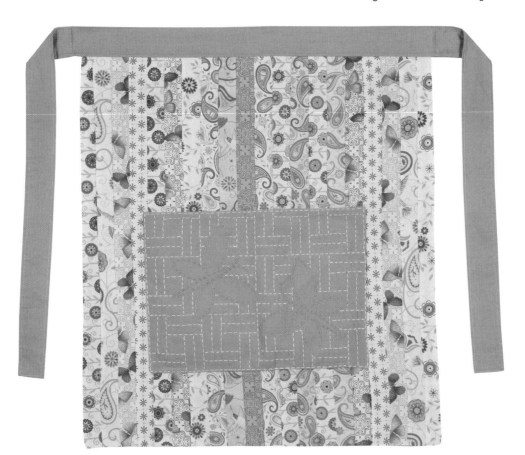

Match on line to make complete pattern.

Spring Butterflies Sashiko Pattern
Transfer and stitch as per instructions

A

Match on line to make complete pattern.

B

Spring Butterflies Sashiko Pattern
Transfer and stitch as per instructions

Palm Leaves Runner

Strip-pieced leaves are the focal point of this lovely runner.
Use 2½-inch strips to create the chevron-shaped leaves.

DESIGN BY CAROL ZENTGRAF

PROJECT SPECIFICATIONS

Skill Level: Beginner
Runner Size: 42" x 17½"

MATERIALS

- 1 strip each 5 different coordinating green fabrics 2½" by fabric width
- 3 B/C strips to match 1 green mottled 2½" by fabric width
- 2 fat quarters to match one green mottled
- 2 fat quarters cream mottled
- Backing 42½" x 18"
- Batting 42½" x 18"
- All-purpose thread to match fabrics
- Green variegated machine-embroidery thread
- 3 (9" x 12") sheets paper-backed fusible web
- Basic sewing tools and supplies

Cutting

1. Cut two 14" x 19½" A rectangles from the cream mottled fat quarters.

2. Cut two 14" x 19½" backing rectangles from the green mottled fat quarters.

3. Cut two 38½" B strips and two 18" C strips from the three green mottled B/C strips.

4. Cut each of the five 2½"-wide green strips into four 10½" lengths.

Completing the Runner

1. Join the two A rectangles on the short ends to make the A background; press seam to one side.

2. Sew a B strip to opposite long sides and C strips to the short ends of A to complete the pieced background; press seams toward B and C strips.

3. Join the two backing rectangles on the short ends, leaving a 3" opening in the center of the seam.

4. Place the pieced background right sides together with the backing; place the batting rectangle on top. Pin and stitch the layers together all around; trim batting close to seam and corners. Turn right side out through the opening in the backing.

5. Press edges flat. Turn the opening edges ¼" to the inside; hand-stitch the opening closed.

6. Stitch in the ditch of seams to hold the layers together using thread to match A.

Completing the Appliqué

1. Sort the 2½" x 10½" strips into four sets of five different-fabric strips each; join the five strips of one set along the 10½" edges to make a strip set. Press seams in one direction. Repeat to make four strip sets, varying color placement of strips. Trim each strip set to 10½" x 10½", if necessary.

2. Place the squares on a cutting surface with the strips running horizontally. Referring to Figure 1 and using a ruler and rotary cutter, cut two of the squares diagonally from the upper left to the lower right corners. Repeat with the second set of squares and cut from the upper right to the lower left corners.

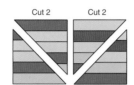

Figure 1

3. To make each pieced chevron square, sew the diagonal edge of a left triangle to the diagonal edge of a right triangle, matching the seams as shown in Figure 2; press seams to one side. Repeat to make three chevron squares.

Figure 2

4. Trace the leaf shape given onto the paper backing of each fusible-web sheet; fuse a sheet to the wrong side of a pieced chevron square, aligning the leaf vein with the center seam of the square as shown in Figure 3. Cut out leaf on traced line. Repeat to cut three leaves.

Figure 3

5. Remove the paper backing from each leaf.

6. Arrange and fuse the leaves onto the A part of the runner referring to the Placement Diagram for positioning.

7. Stitch over the edges of each leaf using a short zigzag stitch with green variegated embroidery thread.

8. Straight-stitch in the ditch of the seams in each leaf using green variegated embroidery thread to finish. ■

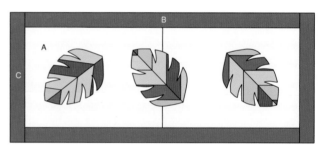

Palm Leaves
Placement Diagram 42" x 17½"

Leaf
Cut 3 as per instructions

Fast Favorite Quilts

Try these extra-fast quilt designs. If they aren't already your favorites, they soon will be. In this chapter, there are 10 easy, but beautiful quilt designs—rustic and masculine designs, stained glass design, lap quilt, bed quilts, shams, super-fast throw, floral quilt and contemporary city wall quilt. Most of them are easy enough for a beginner.

Modern Comfort

Use 10-inch squares cut twice on the diagonal to quickly stitch together this contemporary quilt. When choosing squares, select a package that has half light fabrics and half dark fabrics.

DESIGN BY CONNIE KAUFFMAN

34
10" x 10"

PROJECT SPECIFICATIONS

Skill Level: Beginner
Quilt Size: 52½" x 65½"

MATERIALS

- 13 coordinating light 10" x 10" squares
- 21 coordinating dark 10" x 10" squares
- ½ yard rust tonal
- ⅞ yard green floral
- 1 yard black tonal
- Batting 61" x 74"
- Backing 61" x 74"
- Assorted colors all-purpose thread
- Quilting thread
- 2 (9" x 12") sheets fusible web
- Basic sewing tools and supplies

Cutting

1. Cut 19 dark 10" x 10" squares and 13 light 10" x 10" squares in half on both diagonals to make 76 dark and 52 light A triangles. Select 57 dark and 50 light triangles for quilt; set aside remaining dark triangles for fused triangles.

2. Trim the two remaining dark 10" x 10" squares to make two 5¼" squares; cut the squares in half on one diagonal to make four B triangles.

3. Cut five 2½" by fabric width strips rust tonal. Join strips on short ends to make one long strip; press seams open. Subcut strip into two 53" C strips and two 44" D strips.

4. Cut five 1½" by fabric width strips black tonal. Join strips as in step 3; subcut into two 57" E strips and two 46" F strips.

5. Cut six 2¼" by fabric width strips black tonal for binding.

6. Cut one 7½" by fabric width strip black tonal; subcut strip into four 7½" squares for I.

7. Cut six 4" by fabric width strips green floral. Join strips as in step 3; subcut into two 59" G strips and two 53" H strips.

8. Prepare a template for J using pattern given; trace the J template onto the paper side of the fusible web 16 times as shown in Figure 1. Cut out triangles leaving a small margin around each one; fuse the triangles to the wrong side of the leftover A triangles cut in step 1.

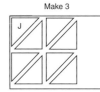
Make 3

Figure 1

9. Cut out the J triangles on the marked lines; remove paper backing.

Completing the Quilt Top

1. Join a light and dark A triangle to make an A-A unit as shown in Figure 2; press seam to one side. Repeat to make 44 A-A units

Figure 2

2. Arrange and join the A-A units in diagonal rows with the remaining A triangles at ends of the rows

and B triangles at two corners referring to Figure 3; press seams in adjoining rows in opposite directions.

Figure 3

3. Join the rows to complete the pieced center; press seams in one direction.

4. Randomly center and fuse a J triangle on the light side of 16 A-A units referring to the Placement Diagram.

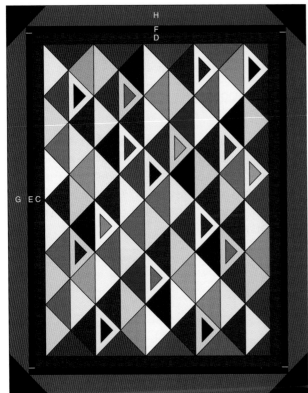

Modern Comfort
Placement Diagram 52½" x 65½"

5. Using a decorative machine stitch and a variety of thread colors, stitch around the edges of each J triangle.

6. Sew C strips to opposite long sides and D strips to the top and bottom of the pieced center; press seams toward C and D strips.

7. Repeat step 6 with the E and F strips and then the G and H strips referring to the Placement Diagram for positioning; press seams toward strips as you sew.

8. Draw a diagonal line from corner to corner on the wrong side of each I square.

9. Place an I square on one corner of the pieced center and stitch on the marked line as shown in Figure 4. Trim seam to ¼" and press I to the right side, again referring to Figure 4.

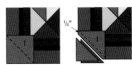

Figure 4

10. Repeat step 9, stitching an I square to each corner to complete the pieced top.

Finishing the Quilt

1. Refer to Finishing Your Quilt on page 176 to sandwich, quilt and bind your quilt to finish. *Note: The quilt shown was machine-quilted in an allover curly design.* ■

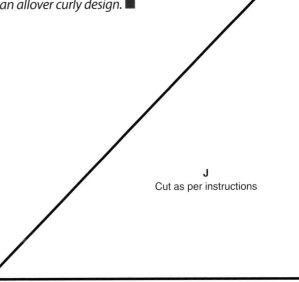

J
Cut as per instructions

Off Kilter

Simple enough for a beginner, this quilt has a clean, modern and masculine look. Switching the fabrics used will quickly change it to a quilt with a soft feminine look.

DESIGNED & QUILTED BY KONDA LUCKAU OF MOOSE ON THE PORCH DESIGNS

PROJECT SPECIFICATIONS

Skill Level: Beginner
Quilt Size: 56" x 67"
Block Size: 7" x 9"
Number of Blocks: 42

MATERIALS

- 11 contemporary print fat quarters
- ⅝ yard charcoal solid
- 1½ yards light gray solid
- Batting 64" x 75"
- Backing 64" x 75"
- Neutral-color all-purpose thread
- Basic sewing tools and supplies

Cutting

1. Cut four 7½" x 9½" A rectangles from each of the 11 fat quarters. Separate into one set of 24 A1 rectangles and one set of 18 A2 rectangles. Set aside two rectangles for another project.

2. Cut four 3¾" by fabric width strips light gray solid; subcut strips into (42) 3¾" B squares.

3. Cut (14) 2½" by fabric width strips light gray solid. Join strips on short ends to make one long strip; press seams open. Subcut strip into seven 63½" C strips and two 56½" D strips.

4. Cut seven 2½" by fabric width binding strips from charcoal solid.

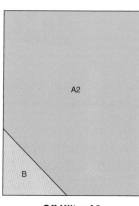

Off Kilter A1
7" x 9" Block
Make 24

Off Kilter A2
7" x 9" Block
Make 18

Completing the Blocks

1. Mark a diagonal line from corner to corner on the wrong side of each B square.

2. Place a B square on one corner of an A1 rectangle and stitch on the marked line as shown in Figure 1; trim seam to ¼" and press B to the right side to complete one Off Kilter A1 block, again referring to Figure 1. Repeat to make a total of 24 Off Kilter A1 blocks.

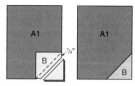

Figure 1

3. Repeat step 2 with A2 rectangles and B squares to complete a total of 18 Off Kilter A2 blocks, referring to Figure 2.

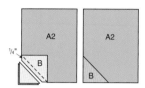

Figure 2

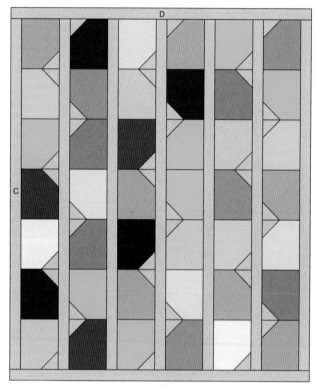

Off Kilter
Placement Diagram 56" x 67"

Completing the Top

1. Select four each A1 and three each A2 blocks; alternate and join these blocks to make a vertical row, referring to Figure 3; press seams in one direction. Repeat to make a total of six vertical rows.

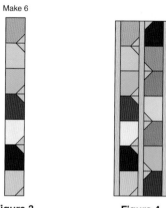

Figure 3   **Figure 4**

2. Join the rows with seven C strips, beginning and ending with a C strip and alternating the direction of rows to make the Off Kilter pattern, referring to Figure 4; press seams toward C strips.

3. Sew a D strip to the top and bottom of the pieced section to complete the quilt top; press seams toward D strips.

Completing the Quilt

1. Refer to Finishing Your Quilt on page 176 to sandwich, quilt and bind your quilt to finish. ■

Jagged Edge

Use one simple block and fat quarters to make this quilt quickly.
Tonal fabrics are used to create the stained glass effect.

DESIGN BY GINA GEMPESAW

QUILTED BY CAROLE WHALING

PROJECT SPECIFICATIONS

Skill Level: Beginner
Quilt Size: 69½" x 69½"
Block Size: 9" x 9"
Number of Blocks: 25

MATERIALS

- 1 fat quarter each purple, red, green, aqua, yellow, coral, magenta, periwinkle and orange mottleds
- ⅔ yard bright green mottled
- 1 yard coordinating print
- 3 yards black tonal
- Backing 78" x 78"
- Batting 78" x 78"
- Black all-purpose thread
- Variegated quilting thread
- Basic sewing tools and supplies

Cutting

1. Cut a total of (32) 8¾" x 8¾" squares from the fat quarter collection and the bright green mottled. Cut each square on both diagonals as shown in Figure 1 to make a total of 128 A triangles.

Figure 1

2. Cut a total of (24) 1½" x 1½" D squares from the remainder of the fat quarters.

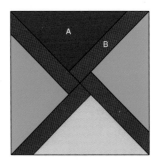

Jagged Edge
9" x 9" Block
Make 25

3. Cut eight 1⅞" x 1⅞" squares from the remainder of the fat quarters; cut each square in half on one diagonal to make (16) E triangles.

4. Cut five 7¼" by fabric width strips black tonal; subcut strips into (128) 1½" B strips. Cut one end of each strip at a 45-degree angle as shown in Figure 2.

Figure 2

5. Cut three 9½" by fabric width strips black tonal; subcut strips into (64) 1½" C sashing strips.

6. Cut seven 2" by fabric width strips black tonal. Join strips on short ends to make one long strip; press seams open. Subcut strip into two 67" J strips and two 70" K strips.

7. Cut seven 2¼" by fabric width strips black tonal for binding.

8. Cut six 1½" by fabric width strips bright green mottled. Join strips on short ends to make one long strip; press seams open. Subcut strip into two 57" F strips and two 59" G strips.

9. Cut seven 4½" by fabric width strips coordinating print. Join strips on short ends to make one long strip; press seams open. Subcut strip into two 59" H strips and two 67" I strips.

Completing the Blocks

1. Sew B to one side of A as shown in Figure 3; press seam toward B. Repeat to make a total of 128 A-B units. Set aside 28 units for side units and corners.

Figure 3   Figure 4

2. Select four A-B units in different colors; join two units as shown in Figure 4. Press seams toward the B strip. Repeat to make a second unit.

3. Join the two units, again referring to Figure 4, to complete one Jagged Edge block; press seam in one direction.

4. Repeat steps 2 and 3 to complete a total of 25 Jagged Edge blocks.

Completing the Quilt Top

1. Select and join two A-B units to make a side unit, again referring to Figure 4. Repeat to make a total of 12 side units.

2. Arrange and join the Jagged Edge blocks and the side and corner units with the C sashing strips, D squares and E triangles in diagonal rows referring to Figure 5; press seams away from the blocks.

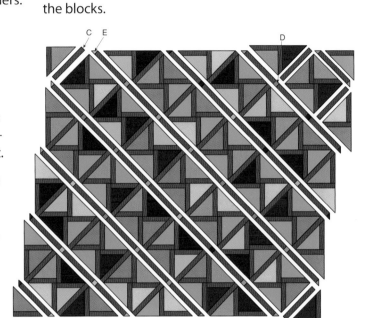

Figure 5

3. Join the block and sashing rows as arranged, and add the corner triangles to complete the pieced center; press seams toward sashing strips.

4. Sew F strips to opposite sides and G strips to the top and bottom of the quilt center; press seams toward F and G strips.

5. Sew H strips to opposite sides and I strips to the top and bottom of the quilt center; press seams toward H and I strips.

6. Sew J strips to opposite sides and K strips to the top and bottom of the quilt center; press seams toward J and K strips.

Completing the Quilt

1. Refer to Finishing Your Quilt on page 176 to sandwich, quilt and bind the quilt. ■

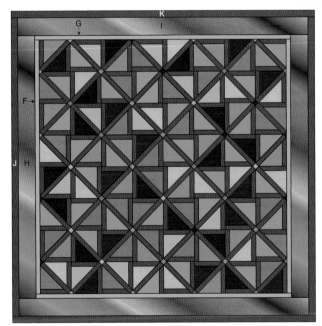

Jagged Edge
Placement Diagram 69½" x 69½"

Mountain Escape

A single cabin lies amidst the trees in this warm quilt. The pieced border lends to the woodsy feel with its dappled colors.

DESIGNED & STITCHED BY GINA GEMPESAW
MACHINE-QUILTED BY CAROLE WHALING

PROJECT NOTE

This project can be completed with fewer than 10 fat quarters—more fabrics are necessary for a scrappy look.

PROJECT SPECIFICATIONS

Skill Level: Easy
Quilt Size: 76" x 88"
Block Size: 10" x 16", 6" x 6"
Number of Blocks: 18, 48

MATERIALS LIST

- 20 fat quarters in various shades of green
- ½ yard dark green mottled for upper tree trunk
- 2½ yards brown mottled
- 3 yards light mottled for background
- 6" x 6" scrap gray mottled
- Batting 84" x 96"
- Backing 84" x 96"
- Neutral-color and gray all-purpose thread
- Quilting thread
- 6" x 6" square lightweight fusible web
- 6" x 6" square tear-off fabric stabilizer (optional)
- Basic sewing tools and supplies

Cutting

Tree Blocks

1. Cut (34) 2½" x 21" strips total from the 20 fat quarter fabrics; subcut strips into (102) 6½" A1 rectangles.

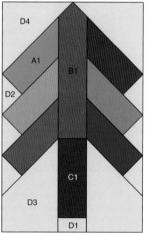

Tree
10" x 16" Block
Make 17

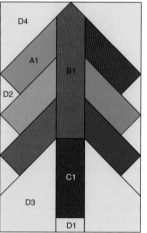

House
10" x 16" Block
Make 1

Nine-Patch
6" x 6" Block
Make 48

2. Cut five 2½" by fabric width strips dark green mottled; subcut strips into (17) 10" B1 rectangles.

3. Cut three 2½" by fabric width strips brown mottled; subcut strips into (17) 6" C1 rectangles.

4. Cut one 2½" by fabric width strip light mottled; subcut strips into (17) 1½" D1 rectangles.

5. Cut three 4⅛" by fabric width strips light mottled; subcut strips into (26) 4⅛" squares. Cut each square on both diagonals to make 102 D2 triangles; set aside the two extra triangles for another project.

6. Cut six 4½" by fabric width strips light mottled; subcut strips into (34) 7" D3 rectangles.

7. Cut three 5⅞" by fabric width strips light mottled; subcut strips into (17) 5⅞" squares. Cut each square in half on one diagonal to make 34 D4 triangles.

House Blocks

1. Row 1 (house base): Select one fat quarter and cut one 2½" x 10½" F rectangle.

2. Row 2: Select a second fat quarter and cut one 2½" x 21" strip; subcut strip into one each 5" K and 2" L rectangle.

3. Row 3: Select a third fat quarter and cut one 2½" x 21" strip; subcut strip into two 2" J rectangles and one 1½" I rectangle.

4. Row 4: Select a fourth fat quarter and cut one 2½" x 21" strip; subcut strip into one 8½" M rectangle.

5. Row 5 (roof) and Row 6 (chimney): Select a fifth fat quarter and cut one 2½" x 21" strip; subcut strip into one 10½" E rectangle and one 1½" x 2" R rectangle.

6. Cut one 2½" by fabric width strip light mottled; subcut strip into one 6½" O rectangle (row 6), one 4½" G door rectangle, one 3" P rectangle (row 6)

and three 2½" H window and roof squares. From the remainder of the strip, cut two 1½" x 6½" N rectangles (sides of house) and one 2" x 1½" Q rectangle (row 6).

7. Cut one 4½" x 10½" S rectangle light mottled.

Background & Borders

1. Cut one 8½" by fabric width strip light mottled; subcut strip into four 10½" D5 rectangles.

2. Cut six 1½" by fabric width U/Y strips light mottled.

3. Cut seven 2" by fabric width T/X strips light mottled.

4. Cut (14) 2½" by fabric width V/W/Z1/Z2 strips brown mottled.

Pieced Border

1. Cut (36) 2½" x 21" A2 strips from the fat quarters.

2. Cut nine 2½" by fabric width strips brown mottled; subcut each strip into two 2½" x 21" C2 strips.

3. Cut eight 2¼" by fabric width brown mottled for binding.

Completing the Tree Blocks

1. Sew one each B1, C1 and D1 rectangles together on short ends to form the tree trunk as shown in Figure 1; press seams toward C1. Repeat to make a total of 17 tree trunks.

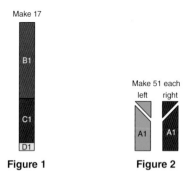

Figure 1

Figure 2

2. Cut a 45-degree angle off of one end of an A1 rectangle to make a right-side branch as shown in Figure 2; repeat with 51 A1 rectangles to make a total of 51 right-side branches.

3. Repeat step 2 to make 51 reverse pieces for the left-side branches again referring to Figure 2.

4. Sew a D2 triangle to the square end of right- and left-side A1 branches as shown in Figure 3.

left   right

D2

Figure 3

Make 17 each
left side   right side

D3

Figure 4

5. Cut a 45-degree angle off of one end of a D3 rectangle as in step 2 to make a left-side base as shown in Figure 4. Repeat to make a total of 17 left-side base pieces.

6. Repeat step 5 to make 17 reverse pieces for the right-side base pieces, again referring to Figure 4.

7. Join three right-side branches with one right-side base to complete the right side of the tree as shown in Figure 5; press seams in one direction.

left side   right side

Figure 5

8. Repeat step 7 with the left-side branches and the left-side base to complete the left side of the tree, again referring to Figure 5.

9. To complete one Tree block, sew a left- and right-side tree unit to opposite long sides of a tree-trunk unit, matching at bottom D1 edges, as shown in Figure 6; press seams toward the center unit.

Figure 6

10. Trim the excess on the top of the tree even with the angle of the branches as shown in Figure 7.

D4

Figure 7   **Figure 8**

11. Sew a D4 triangle to each side of the top angled end of the pieced unit to complete one Tree block, referring to Figure 8; press seams toward D4 triangles.

12. Repeat steps 9–11 to complete a total of 17 Tree blocks.

Completing the House Block

1. Sew Q to R on the long sides and add O to the right end and P to the left end as shown in

Mountain Escape
Placement Diagram 76" x 88"

Figure 9; press seams toward R and then O and P. Add the S rectangle to the top to complete the chimney unit, again referring to Figure 9. Press seam toward S.

Chimney Unit

Figure 9

2. Mark a diagonal line from corner to corner on the wrong side of two H squares. Pin an H square right sides together on each end of E and stitch on the marked lines as shown in Figure 10; trim seams to ¼" and press H to the right side to complete the roof, again referring to Figure 10.

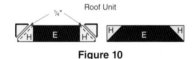

Roof Unit

Figure 10

3. Sew remaining H between I and J, and add K to make the window unit as shown in Figure 11; press seams away from H and toward K.

House Unit

Figure 11   **Figure 12**

4. Sew L to remaining J on short ends; press seam toward J. Sew the L-J unit to the right long edge of G and the window unit to the left long edge of G, add M to the top and N to each side to complete the house unit referring to Figure 12; press seams away from G and toward M and N.

5. To complete the house piecing, sew F to the bottom of the house unit; add the roof unit and then the chimney unit as shown in Figure 13.

Figure 13

6. Trace the smoke shape onto the paper side of the fusible web using the pattern given; cut out the smoke shape leaving a margin all around. Fuse to the wrong side of the gray mottled square; cut out on traced lines. Remove paper backing.

7. Arrange and fuse the smoke shape on the chimney section of the house and into the S background referring to Figure 14.

Figure 14

8. Pin the square of tear-off fabric stabilizer to the wrong side of the pieced house unit beneath the fused smoke piece; using thread to match the smoke piece and a narrow blanket stitch, sew the smoke shape in place. When stitching is complete, remove the stabilizer to complete the House block.

Completing the Nine-Patch Blocks

1. Join one C2 strip with two A2 strips along length to make a C-A-A strip set; repeat to make 12 strip sets. Press seams in one direction.

2. Subcut the C-A-A strip sets into (96) 2½" C-A-A units as shown in Figure 15.

Make 96
2½"

Figure 15

3. Sew a C2 strip between two A2 strips along length to make an A-C-A strip set; repeat to make six strip sets. Press seams in one direction.

4. Subcut the A-C-A strip sets into (48) 2½" A-C-A units as shown in Figure 16.

Make 48
2½"

Figure 16

5. Sew an A-C-A unit between two C-A-A units to make a Nine-Patch block as shown in Figure 17; repeat to make a total of 48 blocks. ***Note:*** *Be sure to sew with the A-C-A seams pressed in the opposite direction from the C-A-A seams.*

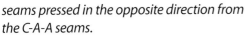

Make 48

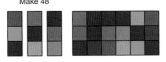

Figure 17

Completing the Quilt Top

1. Join four tree blocks on the 10½" edges to make row 1 as shown in Figure 18; press seams in one direction. Repeat to make rows 3 and 5.

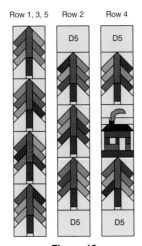

Row 1, 3, 5   Row 2   Row 4

Figure 18

2. Join three Tree blocks on the 10½" edges and add a D5 rectangle to the top and bottom to make row 2, again referring to Figure 18; press seams in one direction.

3. Sew a Tree block to opposite 10½" edges of the House block and add a D5 rectangle to each end to make row 4, again referring to Figure 18.

4. Join the rows in numerical order to complete the quilt center; press seams in one direction.

5. Join the T/X strips on short ends to make one long strip; press seams open. Subcut strip into two 64½" T strips and two 70½" X strips.

Smoke
Cut 1 gray mottled

6. Join the U/Y strips on short ends to make one long strip; press seams open. Subcut strip into two 53½" U strips and two 60½" Y strips.

7. Join the V/W/Z1/Z2 strips on short ends to make one long strip; press seams open. Subcut strip into two 66½" V strips, two 57½" W strips, two 84½" Z1 strips and two 76½" Z2 strips.

8. Sew T strips to opposite long sides and U strips to the top and bottom of the quilt center; press seams toward T and U strips.

9. Repeat step 8 with V and W strips and then X and Y strips, pressing seams toward the V and W strips.

10. Join 12 Nine-Patch blocks, rotating every other block, to make a Nine-Patch strip, again referring to Figure 17; press seams in one direction. Repeat to make a total of four Nine-Patch strips.

11. Sew a Nine-Patch strip to opposite long sides and then to the top and bottom of the pieced center; press seams toward the Nine-Patch strips.

12. Sew a Z1 strip to opposite long sides and the Z2 strips to the top and bottom of the quilt center to complete the quilt top; press seams toward Z1 and Z2 strips.

Completing the Quilt

1. Refer to Finishing Your Quilt on page 176 to sandwich, quilt and bind your quilt to finish. ■

Shadow Play

One package of 1½-inch strips, one package of 2½-inch strips and two charm packs will give you a head start on this lovely quilt. The strips are also used for two of the borders and for the binding.

DESIGN BY JULIE WEAVER

PROJECT SPECIFICATIONS

Skill Level: Beginner
Quilt Size: 52" x 69"
Block Size: 8½" x 8½"
Number of Blocks: 24

MATERIALS

- 80 coordinating 5" x 5" tonal A squares
- 40 coordinating 1½" by fabric width tonal strips
- 40 coordinating 2½" by fabric width tonal strips
- 1 yard cream tonal
- Batting 60" x 75"
- Neutral-color all-purpose thread
- Basic sewing tools and supplies

Cutting

1. Sort fabric strips and squares by color family into 12 stacks of four colors each. Colors should gradate from light to dark in each stack and should contain two 5" x 5" light A squares, one 2½"-wide medium/light strip, and one each 1½"-wide medium/dark and dark strip. **Note:** *You will have extra squares and strips to allow you to have more variety to choose from when selecting for use. Two identical blocks will be made from each stack.*

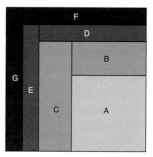

Shadow Play
8½" x 8½" Block
Make 24

2. Cutting one stack of fabric at a time, cut two each 5" B and 7" C strips from the 2½"-wide strips, two each 7" D and 8" E strips from the 1½"-wide medium/dark strips and two each 8" F and 9" G strips from the 1½"-wide dark strips. Separate pieces into two identical stacks, including an A square in each, and pin together for blocks.

3. Repeat step 2 with each of the remaining eleven stacks.

4. Cut (10) 1½" by fabric width H/I/L/M strips cream tonal.

5. Cut six 2½" by fabric width O/P strips cream tonal.

6. Cut a total of (42) 1" x 6" J/K strips from the 1½"-wide medium/dark and dark strips. **Note:** *Strips will need to be trimmed to 1" wide.*

7. Set aside four A squares for border corners. From the remaining A squares and the 2½"-wide medium/light strips, cut a total of (96) 2½" x 5" N rectangles.

8. Cut a total of (35) 9½" rectangles from the 2½"-wide medium/light strips for binding.

Completing the Blocks

1. To complete one Shadow block, sew a B strip to one side of A; press seam toward B. Add C to the left side edge as shown in Figure 1; press seam toward C.

Figure 1   Figure 2

2. Add D to the B side and E to the C side of the A-B-C unit as shown in Figure 2; press seams toward D and then E.

3. Add F to the D side and G to the E side of the pieced unit to complete one block referring to the block drawing; press seams toward F and then G.

4. Repeat steps 1–3 to complete a total of 24 Shadow blocks.

Completing the Top

1. Arrange and join four blocks to make a row as shown in Figure 3; press seams in one direction. Repeat to make a total of six rows.

Figure 3

2. Join the rows referring to the Placement Diagram to complete the quilt center; press seams in one direction.

3. Join the H/I/L/M strips on the short ends to make one long strip; press seams open. Subcut strip into two 51½" H strips, two 36½" I strips, two 54½" L strips and two 39½" M strips.

4. Sew H strips to opposite long sides and I strips to the top and bottom of the quilt center; press seams toward the H and I strips.

5. Referring to Figure 4, join two J/K strips with a diagonal seam; trim seam to ¼" and press open. Continue joining the J/K strips with diagonal seams to make one long strip. Subcut the strip into two 53½" J strips and two 37½" K strips.

Figure 4

6. Sew J strips to opposite long sides and K strips to the top and bottom of the quilt center; press seams toward H and I strips.

7. Sew L strips to opposite long sides and M strips to the top and bottom of the quilt center; press seams toward L and M strips.

8. Join 28 N pieces on the 5" sides to make an N strip; press seams in one direction. Repeat to make a second N strip.

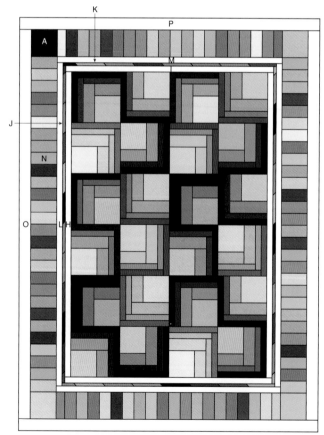

Shadow Play
Placement Diagram 52" x 69"

9. Sew an N strip to opposite long sides of the quilt center. Press seams toward L strips.

10. Repeat step 8 with 20 N pieces to make two short N strips; trim ½" from each end N piece to make a 39½" strip as shown in Figure 5.

Figure 5

11. Sew an A square to each end of each short N strip; press seams toward A. Sew the A-N strips to the top and bottom of the quilt center; press seams toward M strips.

12. Join the O/P strips on the short ends to make one long strip; press seams open. Subcut strip into two 65½" O strips and two 52½" P strips.

13. Sew O strips to opposite long sides and P strips to the top and bottom of the quilt center to complete the quilt top; press seams toward O and P strips.

Completing the Quilt

1. Join the binding strips with diagonal seams as in step 5 in Completing the Top.

2. Refer to Finishing Your Quilt on page 176 to sandwich, quilt and bind your quilt to finish. ◼

Twist & Turn

Even a beginner can make this quilt quickly using precut triangles. Start in the morning and be finished that evening. For a different look, try mixing blacks and whites, or stripes and a single solid color.

DESIGN BY CATHY LEE

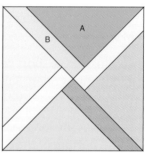

Twist & Turn
8½" x 8½" Block
Make 20

PROJECT SPECIFICATIONS

Skill Level: Beginner
Quilt Size: 40" x 48½"
Block Size: 8½" x 8½"
Number of Blocks: 20

MATERIALS

- 80 coordinating 6" x 6" triangles for A
- ⅓ yard aqua solid
- ¾ yard bubblegum pink solid
- ⅞ yard yellow solid
- Batting 48" x 57"
- Backing 48" x 57"
- Neutral-color all-purpose thread
- Quilting thread
- Basic sewing tools and supplies

Cutting

1. Cut one 8" by fabric width strip each bubblegum pink, aqua and yellow solids; subcut strips into (28) 1½" B strips each fabric. *Note: You will have four extra B strips.*

2. Cut three 3½" by fabric width strips yellow solid. Join on short ends to make one long strip; press seams open. Subcut strips into two 43" C strips.

3. Cut two 3½" x 40½" D strips yellow solid.

4. Cut five 2¼" by fabric width strips bubblegum pink solid for binding.

Completing the Blocks

1. Select four A triangles and four B strips of any color.

2. Align one square end of one B strip with one square end of one A triangle and stitch to make an A-B unit as shown in Figure 1; press seam toward A.

Figure 1

3. Repeat step 2 with the remaining three A and B pieces, sewing B to the same side of each triangle.

4. Join two A-B units as shown in Figure 2; press seam to one side. Repeat to make two units.

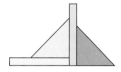

Figure 2

5. Join the two units as shown in Figure 3; press seam in one direction.

Figure 3

6. Using a ruler and rotary cutter, trim excess B and square up to 9" x 9" to complete one Twist & Turn block.

7. Repeat steps 1–6 to complete 20 Twist & Turn blocks.

Completing the Quilt Top

1. Arrange and join four Twist & Turn blocks to make a row; press seams in one direction. Repeat to make five rows, pressing seams in adjoining rows in opposite directions.

2. Join the rows to complete the pieced center; press seams in one direction.

3. Sew a C strip to opposite long sides and D strips to the top and bottom of the pieced center to complete the quilt top; press seams toward strips.

Finishing the Quilt

1. Refer to Finishing Your Quilt on page 176 to sandwich, quilt and bind your quilt to finish. ◼

Twist & Turn
Placement Diagram 40" x 48½"

Sand Scape

This lap quilt has a Southwestern feel with sand-toned light tans and browns, and a touch of turquoise. Using precut 2½-inch strips make this quilt quicker to create and adds a wonderful variety of colors.

DESIGN BY CONNIE KAUFFMAN

PROJECT SPECIFICATIONS

Skill Level: Intermediate
Quilt Size: 58" x 76"

MATERIALS

- 40 coordinated 2½" by fabric width batik strips—2 strips each 20 different batiks
- ¼ yard cream batik
- ⅔ yard purple batik
- ⅞ yard turquoise batik
- 1½ yards medium tan batik
- 1⅔ yards dark brown batik
- Batting 66" x 84"
- Backing 66" x 84"
- Neutral-color all-purpose thread
- 1 package Thangles™ to make at least (44) 2" pieced squares
- Basic sewing tools and supplies

Cutting

1. Cut five 3¾" by fabric width strips medium tan batik. Join strips on short ends to make a long strip; press seams open. Subcut strip into two 54½" K strips and two 43" J strips.

2. Cut five 4½" by fabric width strips medium tan batik. Join strips on short ends to make a long strip; press seams open. Subcut strip into four 46½" F strips.

3. Cut one 4½" by fabric width strip medium tan batik; subcut strip into two 8½" E rectangles and four 4½" G squares.

4. Cut one 2½" by fabric width strip medium tan batik; subcut strips into two 16½" I strips.

5. Cut one 2½" x 21" O strip dark brown batik.

6. Cut two 5½" by fabric width strips dark brown batik; subcut strips into two 10½" U and two 12½" Q strips.

7. Cut three 3½" by fabric width strips dark brown batik; subcut strips into two each 23½" T, 14½" P and 4½" S.

8. Cut four 7½" by fabric width strips dark brown batik; subcut strips into two 36½" R and two 25½" V strips.

9. Cut six 1¼" by fabric width strips turquoise batik. Join strips on short ends to make one long strip; press seams open. Subcut strip into two 44½" N strips and two 61" M strips.

10. Cut one 7⅛" by fabric width strip turquoise batik; subcut strip into four 7⅛" L squares, two 4½" x 4½" H squares and one 4½" x 6½" D rectangle.

11. Cut four 2½" by fabric width strips turquoise batik; subcut one strip into (12) 2½" C squares. Set aside remaining strips for making A-C, B-C and C-O units.

12. Cut seven 2¼" by fabric width strips purple batik for binding.

13. Cut three 2½" by fabric width strips cream batik; subcut one strip into (16) 2½" B1 squares. Set aside remaining two strips for making B-C units.

14. Cut (266) 2½" A1 squares from the 2½"-wide precut strips, removing any turquoise or cream fabrics from the mix. Set aside remaining strips for making A-C units.

Completing the Triangle Units

1. Layer a 2½"-wide turquoise batik strip with a 2½"-wide cream batik strip right sides together; repeat to make a second layered strip.

2. Select 20 Thangles paper patterns and pin the patterns to the fabric strips, aligning outside edges. **Note:** *Refer to product directions for use.*

3. Place a pin in the end of the triangle, and then move fingers along to the solid line and pin. **Note:** *The solid line is the cutting line when stitching is complete.*

4. Continue pinning in each triangle and through each solid line along the length of the strips.

5. Sew through all layers on the dotted lines using a regular stitch length (2mm or 12 per inch) with a No. 70 or 80 sewing needle.

6. Cut apart on the solid lines; trim away the one pointed dog-ear.

7. Flip the unit over with fabric side up; open and press with paper still attached.

8. Remove the paper after pressing to complete the 20 B-C units as shown in Figure 1.

Make 20   Make 8   Make 16

Figure 1

9. Repeat Steps 1–8 with a turquoise C and O strip to make eight C-O units, again referring to Figure 1.

Alternate Method

If you prefer to make the B-C units without using the Thangles product, cut one 2⅞" x 42" strip each fabrics A, B and O and two 2⅞" x 42" strips fabric C. Subcut the O strip into four 2⅞" squares, the A strip into eight 2⅞" squares, the B strip into (10) 2⅞" squares and the C strips into (22) 2⅞" squares. Cut the squares in half on one diagonal to make four O, 16 A, 20 B and 44 C and O triangles.

Join the triangles to make eight C-O, 16 A-C and 20 B-D units referring to Figure 1.

---

10. Repeat steps 1–8 with a turquoise C strip and remaining set-aside precut strips from step 14 of Cutting, to make 16 A-C units, again referring to Figure 1.

Completing the Top

1. Select, arrange and join five A1 squares and one B-C unit to make a strip as shown in Figure 2; press seams in one direction. Repeat to make two strips.

2. Repeat step 1 with B-C units reversed to make two reversed strips, again referring to Figure 2.

A1 Make 2

Make 2 reversed

Make 2

Figure 2   **Figure 3**

3. Join two of the strips as shown in Figure 3; press seam to one side. Repeat. Join these two strips with the D rectangle and two E rectangles to make the center row as shown in Figure 4; press seams toward D and E. Sew an F strip to opposite long sides of the center row, again referring to Figure 4; press seams toward F strips.

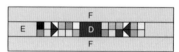

Figure 4

4. Join 13 A1 squares with two B1 squares, two B-C units and two A-C units to make a row as shown in Figure 5; press seams in one direction. Repeat to make two rows.

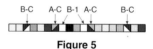

B-C   A-C B-1 A-C   B-C

Figure 5

5. Repeat step 4, rearranging the squares and units as shown in Figure 6, to make 2 rows.

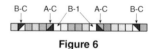

B-C   A-C   B-1   A-C   B-C

Figure 6

6. Join one of each row and add G to make a center side row as shown in Figure 7; press seams toward G. Repeat to make a second center side row.

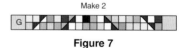

Make 2

Figure 7

7. Sew a center side row to each F side of the center row as shown in Figure 8, making sure the center side rows are reversed; press seams toward F strips.

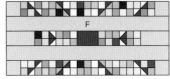

Figure 8

8. Draw a diagonal line from corner to corner on the wrong side of each H square. Place an H square on one end of each remaining F strip and stitch on the marked line as shown in Figure 9; trim seam to ¼" and press H to the right side, again referring to Figure 9.

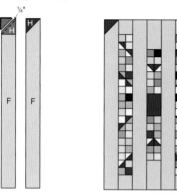

Figure 9

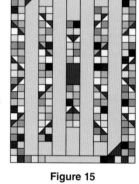

Figure 10

9. Sew an F-H strip to each side of the pieced center referring to Figure 10 for positioning of the strips; press seams toward the F-H strips.

10. Join 17 A1 squares, two B1 squares, two B-C units and two A-C units to make a strip as shown in Figure 11; repeat to make two strips. Press seams in one direction.

11. Repeat step 10, rearranging the A1 and B1 squares and B-C and A-C units to make two strips, again referring to Figure 11; press seams in one direction.

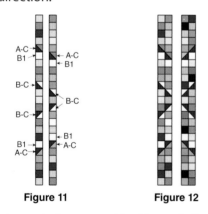

A-C
B1
A-C
B1
B-C
B-C
B-C
B1
B1
A-C
A-C

Figure 11   **Figure 12**

12. Join a strip from step 10 with a strip from step 11 to make a side strip as shown in Figure 12; repeat to make two side strips. Press seams to one side.

13. Sew side strips to opposite long sides of the quilt center; press seams toward F-H strips.

14. Referring to Figure 13, join one C square and four A1 squares to make an end unit; press seams in one direction. Repeat to make two end units.

C Make 2

Figure 13   **Figure 14**

15. Join the two end units with I to make a top strip as shown in Figure 14; press seams toward I.

16. Repeat steps 14 and 15 to make a bottom strip.

17. Sew the strips made in steps 14–16 to the top and bottom of the pieced center referring to Figure 15; press seams to one side.

18. Join 16 A1 squares and add a C square to each end to make a top strip as shown in Figure 16; press seams in one direction. Repeat to make a bottom strip. Sew a strip to the top and bottom of the pieced center; press seams to one side.

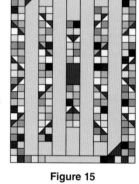

Figure 15

Make 2

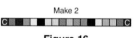

Figure 16

19. Sew a K strip to opposite long sides and J strips to the top and bottom of the pieced center; press seams toward J and K strips.

20. Draw a diagonal line from corner to corner on the wrong side of each L square. Place an L square on each J/K corner of the quilt top and stitch on the marked line as shown in Figure 17; trim seam to ¼" and press L to the right side, again referring to Figure 17.

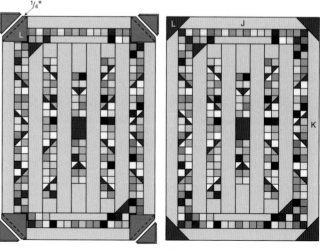

Figure 17

21. Sew an M strip to opposite long sides and N strips to the top and bottom of the pieced center; press seams toward M and N strips.

22. Join one C-O unit with 12 A1 squares as shown in Figure 18; press seam in one direction. Repeat with one C-O unit and six A1 squares, again referring to Figure 18.

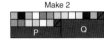
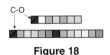

Figure 18   Figure 19

23. Sew a P strip to the six A1 squares and add Q to the C-O end as shown in Figure 19; press seams toward P and Q. Add the 12 A1 unit to the six A1 side to make a side bottom strip, again referring to Figure 19.

24. Sew an R strip to the C-O end of the side bottom strip to complete the side border strip referring to Figure 20; press seam toward R.

Figure 20

25. Repeat steps 22–24 to make a second side border strip. Sew these strips to opposite long sides of the pieced center referring to the Placement Diagram for positioning; press seams to one side.

26. Join four A1 squares with one C-O unit and U to make a U unit as shown in Figure 21; press seams in one direction, then toward U. Repeat to make two U units.

Figure 21   Figure 22

27. Join eight A1 squares with one C-O unit and one C square to make a long strip as shown in Figure 22; press seams in one direction.

28. Repeat step 27 with nine A1 squares and one C square, again referring to Figure 22.

29. Join the strips made in steps 27 and 28 and add S and then T to make a T unit as shown in

Figure 23; press seams in one direction, toward S and then T.

Figure 23

30. Repeat steps 27–29 to make two T units.

31. Join one T unit with one U unit and a V strip to make the top strip as shown in Figure 24; press seams toward the U unit and V. Repeat to make the bottom strip.

Figure 24

32. Sew the top strip to the top and the bottom strip to the bottom of the pieced center to complete the quilt top, referring to the Placement Diagram for positioning; press seams to one side.

Completing the Quilt

1. Refer to Finishing Your Quilt on page 176 to sandwich, quilt and bind your quilt to finish. ■

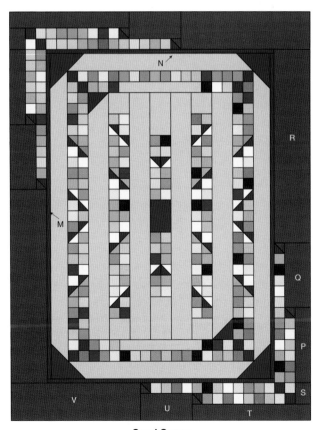

Sand Scape
Placement Diagram 58" x 76"

12

21" x 18"

Fancy Flowers

Use two different blocks to frame your favorite floral fabrics and create a quilt with lots of color and energy. This is inside gardening at its best!

DESIGN BY JUDITH SANDSTROM

PROJECT SPECIFICATIONS

Skill Level: Intermediate
Quilt Size: 66" x 90"
Block Size: 12" x 12"
Number of Blocks: 35

MATERIALS

- 1 fat quarter of each of the following: 6 different orchid prints, and turquoise, light green, brown, dark pink, dark green and yellow prints
- ⅓ yard yellow dragonfly print
- 1 yard dark green beetle print
- 1¼ yards hot pink beetle print
- 2¼ yards cream dragonfly print
- Batting 74" x 98"
- Backing 74" x 98"
- Neutral-color all-purpose thread
- Quilting thread
- Basic sewing tools and supplies

Cutting

1. Cut one 6½" x 21" strip each orchid print fat quarter; subcut strips into three 6½" A squares each print.

2. Cut two 5⅛" x 21" strips each orchid print fat quarter; subcut strips into six 5⅛" squares and one 3½" x 3½" K square. Cut each 5⅛" square in half on one diagonal to make 12 H triangles each print.

3. Cut six 1½" x 21" B strips from each of the remaining fat quarters.

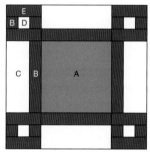

Framed Flowers
12" x 12" Block
Make 18

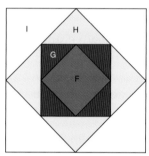

Square-in-a-Square
12" x 12" Block
Make 17

4. Cut four 1½" x 21" strips from each of the remaining fat quarters; subcut strips into (24) 3½" E rectangles of each fabric.

5. Cut two 3⅞" by fabric width strips dark green beetle print; subcut strips into (14) 3⅞" squares. Cut each square in half on one diagonal to make 28 G triangles.

6. Cut eight 2¼" by fabric width strips dark green beetle print for binding.

7. Cut two 3⅞" by fabric width strips yellow dragonfly print; subcut strips into (20) 3⅞" squares. Cut each square in half on one diagonal to make 40 G triangles.

8. Cut three 4¾" by fabric width strips hot pink beetle print; subcut strips into (17) 4¾" F squares.

9. Cut four 3½" x 41" J strips hot pink beetle print.

10. Cut three 3½" by fabric width strips hot pink beetle print. Join on short ends to make one long strip; press seams open. Subcut strip into two 60½" L strips.

11. Cut (12) 2½" by fabric width strips cream dragonfly print; subcut strips into (24) 21" C strips.

12. Cut three 1½" by fabric width strips cream dragonfly print; subcut strips into six 21" D strips.

13. Cut six 6⅞" by fabric width strips cream dragonfly print; subcut strips into (34) 6⅞" square. Cut each square in half on one diagonal to make 68 I triangles.

Completing the Framed Flowers Blocks

1. Select all B strips and E rectangles of one fabric, and all A squares of one orchid print.

2. Sew a B strip to a C strip with right sides together along length to make a B-C strip set; press seam toward B strip. Repeat to make four B-C strip sets.

3. Subcut the B-C strip sets into (12) 6½" B-C units as shown in Figure 1.

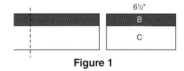

Figure 1

4. Sew a D strip between two B strips with right sides together along length to make a B-D-B strip set; press seams toward B strips.

5. Subcut the B-D-B strip set into (12) 1½" B-D-B units as shown in Figure 2.

Figure 2

Figure 3

6. Sew an E rectangle to opposite sides of a B-D-B unit to make a corner unit as shown in Figure 3; press seams toward the E rectangles. Repeat to make 12 corner units.

7. To complete one Framed Flowers block, sew a B-C unit to opposite sides of an A square to make the center row as shown in Figure 4; press seams toward the B-C unit.

Figure 4

8. Sew a corner unit to opposite ends of a B-C unit to make a top/bottom strip as shown in Figure 5; press seams toward the B-C unit. Repeat to make a second strip.

Figure 5

9. Sew a top/bottom strip to the remaining sides of the center row as shown in Figure 6 to complete one Framed Flowers block; press seams toward the strips.

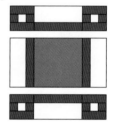

Figure 6

10. Repeat steps 6–8 to complete a total of three Framed Flowers blocks of one fabric combination.

11. Repeat steps 1–10 to complete three blocks each of five more combinations to make 18 blocks total.

Completing the Square-in-a-Square Blocks

1. To complete one Square-in-a-Square block, select four each matching G and matching H triangles.

2. Sew a G triangle to each side of an F square as shown in Figure 7; press seams toward G.

Figure 7

3. Add an H triangle to each side of the F-G unit; press seams toward H.

4. Sew an I triangle to each side of the pieced unit to complete one block; press seams toward I triangles.

5. Repeat steps 1–4 to complete a total of 17 Square-in-a-Square blocks. Discard remaining H triangles.

Completing the Quilt Top

1. Join two Framed Flowers blocks and three Square-in-a-Square blocks to make an X row as shown in Figure 8; press seams toward the Square-in-a-Square blocks. Repeat to make three X rows.

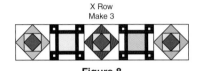

X Row
Make 3

Figure 8

2. Join two Square-in-a-Square blocks and three Framed Flowers blocks to make a Y row as shown in Figure 9; press seams toward the Square-in-a-Square blocks. Repeat to make four Y rows.

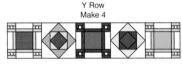

Y Row
Make 4

Figure 9

3. Join the X and Y rows to complete the pieced center referring to the Placement Diagram for positioning; press seams in one direction.

4. Join two J strips with a K square to make a J-K side strip; press seams toward the J strips. Repeat to make two J-K side strips. Sew a strip to opposite long sides of the pieced center; press seams toward strips.

5. Sew a K square to each end of each L strip to make the top strip; press seams away from K. Repeat to make the bottom strip. Sew the strips to the top and bottom of the pieced center to complete the quilt top; press seams toward strips.

Finishing the Quilt

1. Refer to Finishing Your Quilt on page 176 to sandwich, quilt and bind your quilt to finish. ◼

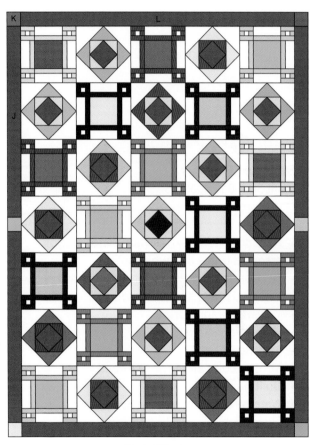

Fancy Flowers
Placement Diagram 66" x 90"

Running Stripes Quilt & Shams

Using two sizes of precut strips of fabric will definitely jump-start this beginner quilt. Adjusting the size to fit your bed is also very easy.

DESIGN BY CAROL ZENTGRAF

Quilt

PROJECT SPECIFICATIONS

Skill Level: Beginner
Quilt Size: 84" x 95½"

MATERIALS

- 72 coordinating 2½" by fabric width strips assorted prints and white solid
- 38 coordinating 1½" by fabric width strips assorted prints and white solid
- 1⅞ yards orange print
- High-loft batting 92" x 103"
- Backing 92" x 103"
- Neutral-color all-purpose thread
- Quilting thread
- Water-erasable marker or pencil
- Clear ruler
- Basic sewing tools and supplies

Cutting

1. Cut seven 5" by fabric width strips orange print. Join strips on short ends to make one long strip; press seams open. Subcut strip into two 91½" A strips and one 84½" B strip.

2. Cut nine 2½" by fabric width strips orange print for binding.

Completing the Quilt Top

1. On a large, flat surface, arrange (36) 2½"-wide strips and (19) 1½"-wide strips, alternating colors and strip widths as desired. When satisfied with the arrangement, pick up the strips and stack in the order of arrangement. Repeat to make a second stack of strips.

2. Join the first two strips in one stack with right sides together along length; press seam to one side. Continue to add strips, pressing seams in the same direction, until you have used all of the strips in one stack. Repeat with the second stack of strips.

3. Referring to Figure 1, cut each of the strip sets into three 13"-wide panels to total six strip panels.

4. Lay the six strip panels on a flat surface and turn every other panel upside down so the colors are reversed referring to the Placement Diagram for positioning of strips.

13"

Figure 1

5. Join the panels as arranged, aligning seams that meet. **Note:** *Because the seam allowances will be pressed in opposite directions on adjacent panels, they should nest together when sewn. Press seams to one side.*

6. Using a water-erasable marker or pencil, and a clear ruler, mark vertical quilting lines on each pieced panel evenly spacing them slightly over 3" apart as shown in Figure 2.

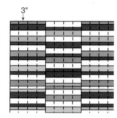

Figure 2

7. Sew A strips to opposite long sides and a B strip to the bottom to complete the quilt top; press seams toward A and B strips.

Completing the Quilt

1. Refer to Finishing Your Quilt on page 176 to sandwich, quilt and bind your quilt to finish. Quilt on marked lines or as desired.

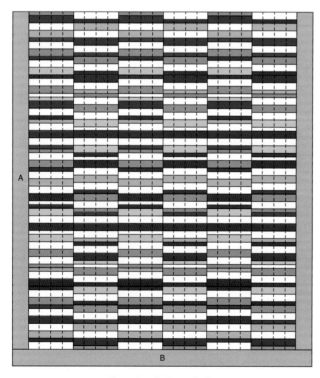

Running Stripes Quilt
Placement Diagram 84" x 95½"

Pillow Shams

PROJECT SPECIFICATIONS

Skill Level: Beginner
Sham Size: 27" x 23"

MATERIALS

Makes 2 shams
- 6 coordinating 2½" by fabric width strips assorted prints and white solid
- 4 coordinating 1½" by fabric width strips assorted prints and white solid
- ⅞ yard orange print
- 1⅝ yards muslin
- 2 rectangles low-loft batting 28" x 24"
- 4 backing rectangles 23½" x 17"
- Neutral-color all-purpose thread
- Quilting thread
- Basic sewing tools and supplies

Cutting

1. Cut two 4" by fabric width strips orange print; subcut strips into four 16½" C strips.

2. Cut four 4" x 27½" D strips orange print.

3. Cut two 30" x 26" rectangles muslin.

Completing the Sham Tops

1. On a large, flat surface, arrange the 2½"-wide strips and the 1½"-wide strips, alternating colors and strip widths as desired. When satisfied with the arrangement, pick up the strips and stack in the order of arrangement.

2. Join the first two strips in the stack with right sides together along length; press seam to one side. Continue to add strips, pressing seams in the same direction, until you have used all of the strips in the stack.

3. Referring to Figure 3, cut the strip set into two 16½" x 20½" panels.

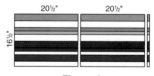

Figure 3

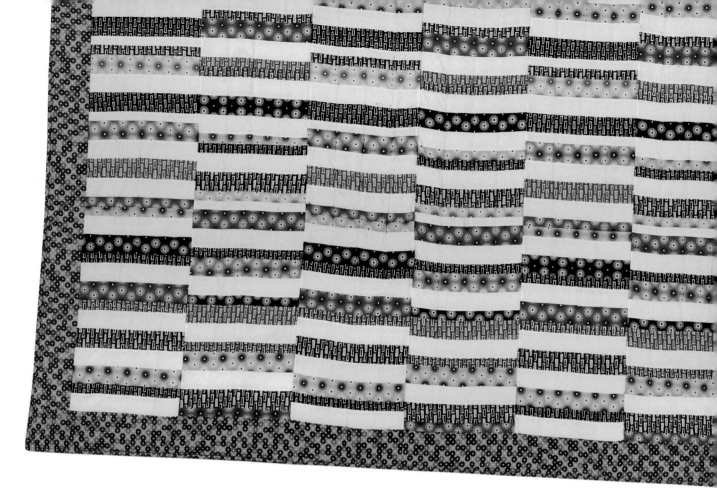

4. Using a water-erasable marker or pencil, and a clear ruler, mark vertical quilting lines on each pieced panel evenly spacing them slightly over 3" apart as shown in Figure 4.

Figure 4

5. Sew C strips to opposite short sides and a D strips to opposite long sides of each panel to complete the sham tops; press seams toward C and D strips to complete the sham tops.

Completing the Shams

1. Sandwich one piece of batting between one sham top and one muslin rectangle; pin or baste to hold.

2. Quilt on the marked lines. When quilting is complete, trim edges even.

3. Repeat steps 1 and 2 with the second sham top.

4. Fold over ¼" on one 23½" edge of each backing piece; fold over ¼" again and stitch to hem.

5. Pin two hemmed backing rectangles right sides together with each quilted sham top, overlapping hemmed edges referring to Figure 5; stitch all around.

Figure 5

6. Turn shams right side out through back openings and press edges flat to finish. ■

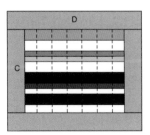

Running Stripes Sham
Placement Diagram 27" x 23"

High-Rise Quarters

Build the image of a contemporary city building out of fat quarters for a quilt that is as striking as it is easy.

DESIGN BY ANN D. HANSEN
MACHINE-QUILTED BY DIANE LIDDELL

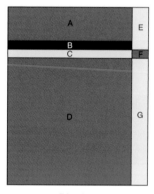

Block 1
17" x 21" Block
Make 3

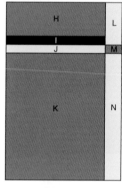

Block 2
14" x 21" Block
Make 3

PROJECT SPECIFICATIONS

Skill Level: Beginner
Quilt Size: 49" x 70"
Block Sizes: 17" x 21", 14" x 21" and 11" x 21"
Number of Blocks: 3 each size

MATERIALS

- 9 print fat quarters
- 3 solid fat quarters
- ½ yard black solid
- ⅔ yard bright colors on brown print
- Batting 57" x 78"
- Backing 57" x 78"
- All-purpose thread to match fabrics
- Quilting thread
- Basic sewing tools and supplies

Cutting

Note: *Before cutting, arrange prints by row and order so you cut the right sizes.*

1. To make Block 1, select three print fat quarters. Cut one each of the following from each fat quarter: 15½" x 4½" A strip, 15½" x 15½" D square and 2½" x 1½" F rectangle.

2. To make Block 2, select three print fat quarters. Cut one each of the following from each fat quarter: 12½" x 4½" H strip, 12½" x 15½" K strip and 2½" x 1½" M rectangle.

3. To make Block 3, cut one each of the following from each of the remaining three print fat quarters: 9½" x 4½" O strip, 9½" x 15½" R strip and 2½" x 1½" T rectangle.

4. Cut three 1½" x 21" strips from each of the three solid fat quarters; subcut one each of the following sizes from each solid: 15½" C strip, 12½" J strip and 9½" Q strip.

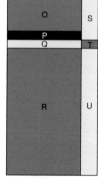

Block 3
11" x 21" Block
Make 3

5. Cut three 2½" x 21" strips from the remainder of the three solid fat quarters used in step 4; subcut three each of the following sizes from each solid: 5½" (label one of each solid E, L and S) and 15½" (label one of each solid G, N and U).

6. Cut four 1½" by fabric width strips black solid; subcut strips into three each 15½" B strips, 12½" I strips and 9½" P strips.

7. Cut three 1½" by fabric width V/X strips black solid.

8. Cut six 2¼" by fabric width strips black solid for binding.

9. Cut three 6½" by fabric width W/Y strips bright colors on brown print.

Completing the Blocks

1. Sew A to B to C to D along the 15½" edges; press seams toward B and C strips.

2. Sew F between E and G; press seams away from F.

3. Sew the E-F-G strip to the A-B-C-D unit to complete Block 1 referring to the block drawing; press seams toward the E-F-G strip.

4. Repeat steps 1–3 to complete three different color combinations of Block 1, referring to the Placement Diagram for color positioning.

5. Sew H to I to J to K along the 12½" edges; press seams toward I and J strips.

6. Sew M between L and N; press seams away from M.

7. Sew the L-M-N strip to the H-I-J-K unit to complete Block 2 referring to the block drawing; press seams toward the L-M-N strip.

8. Repeat steps 5–7 to complete three different color combinations of Block 2, referring to the Placement Diagram for color positioning.

9. Sew O to P to Q to R along the 9½" edges; press seams toward P and Q strips.

High-Rise Quarters
Placement Diagram 49" x 70"

10. Sew T between S and U; press seams away from T.

11. Sew the S-T-U strip to the O-P-Q-R unit to complete Block 3 referring to the block drawing; press seams toward the S-T-U strips.

12. Repeat steps 9–11 to complete three different color combinations of Block 3, referring to the Placement Diagram for color positioning.

Completing the Top

1. Select one each Blocks 1, 2 and 3 with same-color solid pieces and join in numerical order to make a row as shown in Figure 1; press seams in one direction. Repeat to make three rows, pressing seams in adjacent rows in opposite directions.

Figure 1

2. Join the rows to complete the pieced section; press seams in one direction.

3. Join the V/X strips on short ends to make one long strip; press seams open. Subcut strip into one 63½" V strip and one 49½" X strip.

4. Join the W/Y strips on short ends to make one long strip; press seams open. Subcut strip into one 63½" W strip and one 49½" Y strip.

5. Sew a V strip to a W strip along length; press seam toward the W strip.

6. Sew the V-W strip to the right long side of the pieced section; press seam toward the V-W strip.

7. Sew the X strip to the Y strip along length; press seam toward the Y strip.

8. Sew the X-Y strip to the bottom edge of the pieced section to complete the pieced top; press seam toward the X-Y strips.

Finishing the Quilt

1. Prepare the finished top for quilting, quilt and bind referring to Finishing Your Quilt on page 176 to finish. ■

Special Thanks

Please join us in thanking the talented designers below.

Julia Dunn
Quick Cake Stand Runner, 10
Charming Ohio Star Throw, 18

Susan Fletcher
Fresh Furoshiki Fabric Gift Wrap, 57
Spring Butterflies Apron, 124

Traci Garner
Simple Log Cabin Throw, 28

Gina Gempesaw
Jagged Edge, 141
Mountain Escape, 144

Ann Hansen
High-Rise Quarters, 170

Reeze L. Hanson
Hooray for Holidays, 80

Julie Higgins
With a Twist of Orange, 120

Connie Kauffman
Americana Summer, 73
Fern Place Mats, 112
Modern Comfort, 135
Sand Scape, 157

Cathy Lee
Twist & Turn, 154

Konda Luckau
Off Kilter, 138

Chris Malone
Christmas Fun, 76
Climbing Vines & Squares, 88
Black Cats & Spiders, 92
Chicken Kitchen Table Set, 101
Charmed Runner & Coasters, 108

Connie Rand
Sparkling Stars, 7
Extra X's Bed Runner, 98

Judith Sandstrom
Fancy Flowers, 162

Christine Schultz
Quilt-As-You-Go Doggie Coat, 48

Karla Schulz
Dream Windows Nap Quilt, 25

Wendy Sheppard
Spring Nesting, 54
French Bouquet, 60
Lollipop Spring, 116

Avis Shirer
Wild Goose Chase in Red, 14
Cheerful Blooms & Buttons, 83

Carolyn S. Vagts
Blissful Bag, 32

Julie Weaver
Shadow Play, 150

Johanna Wilson
Friends Together, 22

Carol Zentgraf
Summer Sunflower
  Tote & Wallet, 38
Hibiscus Blooms Pillow, 45
Jolly Jelly Stockings, 66
Palm Leaves Runner, 130
Running Stripes Quilt
  and Shams, 166

Fabric & Supplies

Page 10: Quick Cake Stand Runner—Saltbox Harvest Layer Cake collection by Deb Strain for Moda, and Thangles paper templates for 2" finished half-square triangles.

Page 18: Charming Ohio Star Throw—Charm squares from the Autumn Journey fabric collection by Kansas Troubles Quilters for Moda, and Marbles fabric collection by Moda.

Page 28: Simple Log Cabin Throw—Park Avenue fabric collection by 3 Sisters for Moda.

Page 32: Blissful Bag—Berry Bliss Bali Pop from Hoffman Fabrics, and Bosal No. 325 fusible fleece.

Page 38: Summer Sunflower Tote & Wallet—Fusion and Artisan batiks from Robert Kaufman, Fabric-Tac permanent fabric adhesive from Beacon Adhesives, and Steam-A-Seam 2 fusible web from The Warm Company.

Page 45: Hibiscus Blooms Pillow—Steam-A-Seam 2 from The Warm Company, and Poly-fil Low-Loft batting and Polyester Fiberfill from Fairfield Processing Corp.

Page 54: Spring Nestings—Jelly Roll and Layer Cake from the Tweet Bird collection by Moda, Tuscany Silk batting from Hobbs, piecing and quilting thread from Aurifil, silk quilting thread for tree from YLI, and Steam-A-Seam 2 fusible web from The Warm Company.

Page 57: Fresh Furoshiki Gift Wrap—Fresh fabric collection by Deb Strain for Moda.

Page 60: French Bouquet—Fancy Hill Farm fabric collection from RJR Fabrics, Tuscany wool batting from Hobbs, Steam-A-Seam 2 fusible web from The Warm Company, and Silk 100 quilting thread from YLI.

Page 66: Jolly Jelly Stockings— Sparkle All the Way fabric collection from Robert Kaufman, Fabric-Tac permanent fabric adhesive from Beacon Adhesives, Ball Fringe Trim No. RD4432 from Expo International, and Steam-A-Seam 2 fusible web from The Warm Company.

Page 73: Americana Summer—Steam-A-Seam 2 and Warm & Natural batting from The Warm Company, and So Fine!, Bottom Line and King Tut threads from Superior Threads.

Page 76: Christmas Fun—12 Days of Christmas fabric collection by Kate Spain for Moda.

Page 80: Hooray for Holidays—Fat quarters from the 12 Day of Christmas fabric collection by Kate Spain for Moda.

Page 88: Climbing Vines & Squares—Lakeside Resort fabric collection by Holly Taylor for Moda.

Page 92: Black Cats & Spiders—Frolic fabric collection by Sandy Gervais for Moda.

Page 98: Extra X's Bed Runner—Star Machine Quilting Thread from Coats.

Page 101: Chicken Kitchen Table Set—Insulbright batting from The Warm Company.

Page 108: Charmed Runner & Coasters—Fresh Cottons by Joanna Figueroa, Figure Tree & Co. for Moda.

Page 112: Fern Place Mats—Warm & Natural cotton batting and Steam-A-Seam 2 fusible web from The Warm Company, and Cotton Blendable thread from Sulky.

Page 116: Lollipop Spring—Tweet Tweet fabric collection from Moda.

Page 124: Spring Butterflies Apron—Fresh fabric collection by Deb Strain for Moda.

Page 130: Palm Leaves Runner—Poly-Fil Low-Loft Batting from Fairfield Processing Corp., fabrics from Robert Kaufman Fabrics, and Steam-A-Seam 2 from The Warm Company.

Page 135: Modern Comfort—Sulky(R) Cotton Blendable Thread™ used for decorative stitching, and Warm & Natural cotton batting and Steam-a-Seam 2 from The Warm Company.

Page 141: Jagged Edge—Oodles of Doodles and Rhapsodie Coloree II fabric collections by Ricky Tims for Red Rooster Fabrics.

Page 150: Shadow Play—Hobbs Thermore Batting.

Page 154: Twist & Turn—Swanky Turnovers and Bella solids from Moda.

Page 157: Sand Scape—Sahara Desert Strip-Tease Bun from Island Batiks, Thangles paper-piecing product, Warm & Natural batting from The Warm Company, and King Tut and So Fine! Threads from Superior Threads.

Page 162: Fancy Flowers—Wild Orchids fabric collection from Northcott.

Page 166: Running Stripes Quilt & Shams—Groove fabric collection from Robert Kaufman, and Poly-fil High-Loft and Low-Loft battings from Fairfield Processing Corp.

Photo Index

Finishing Your Quilt

When you have completed the quilt top as instructed with patterns, finish your quilt with these four easy steps.

1. Sandwich the batting between the completed top and prepared backing; pin or baste layers together to hold. ***Note:*** *If using basting spray to hold layers together, refer to instructions on the product container for use.*

2. Quilt as desired by hand or machine; remove pins or basting. Trim excess backing and batting even with quilt top.

3. Join binding strips on short ends to make one long strip. Fold the strip in half along length with wrong sides together; press.

4. Sew binding to quilt edges, mitering corners and overlapping ends. Fold binding to the back side and stitch in place to finish. ■

Metric Conversion Charts

Metric Conversions

Canada/U.S. Measurement		Multiplied by		Metric Measurement
yards	x	.9144	=	metres (m)
yards	x	91.44	=	centimetres (cm)
inches	x	2.54	=	centimetres (cm)
inches	x	25.40	=	millimetres (mm)
inches	x	.0254	=	metres (m)

Canada/U.S. Measurement		Multiplied by		Metric Measurement
centimetres	x	.3937	=	inches
metres	x	1.0936	=	yards

Standard Equivalents

Canada/U.S. Measurement		Metric Measurement		
⅛ inch	=	3.20 mm	=	0.32 cm
¼ inch	=	6.35 mm	=	0.635 cm
⅜ inch	=	9.50 mm	=	0.95 cm
½ inch	=	12.70 mm	=	1.27 cm
⅝ inch	=	15.90 mm	=	1.59 cm
¾ inch	=	19.10 mm	=	1.91 cm
⅞ inch	=	22.20 mm	=	2.22 cm
1 inch	=	25.40 mm	=	2.54 cm
⅛ yard	=	11.43 cm	=	0.11 m
¼ yard	=	22.86 cm	=	0.23 m
⅜ yard	=	34.29 cm	=	0.34 m
½ yard	=	45.72 cm	=	0.46 m
⅝ yard	=	57.15 cm	=	0.57 m
¾ yard	=	68.58 cm	=	0.69 m
⅞ yard	=	80.00 cm	=	0.80 m
1 yard	=	91.44 cm	=	0.91 m
1⅛ yards	=	102.87 cm	=	1.03 m
1¼ yards	=	114.30 cm	=	1.14 m

Canada/U.S. Measurement		Metric Measurement		
1⅜ yards	=	125.73 cm	=	1.26 m
1½ yards	=	137.16 cm	=	1.37 m
1⅝ yards	=	148.59 cm	=	1.49 m
1¾ yards	=	160.02 cm	=	1.60 m
1⅞ yards	=	171.44 cm	=	1.71 m
2 yards	=	182.88 cm	=	1.83 m
2⅛ yards	=	194.31 cm	=	1.94 m
2¼ yards	=	205.74 cm	=	2.06 m
2⅜ yards	=	217.17 cm	=	2.17 m
2½ yards	=	228.60 cm	=	2.29 m
2⅝ yards	=	240.03 cm	=	2.40 m
2¾ yards	=	251.46 cm	=	2.51 m
2⅞ yards	=	262.88 cm	=	2.63 m
3 yards	=	274.32 cm	=	2.74 m
3⅛ yards	=	285.75 cm	=	2.86 m
3¼ yards	=	297.18 cm	=	2.97 m
3⅜ yards	=	308.61 cm	=	3.09 m
3½ yards	=	320.04 cm	=	3.20 m
3⅝ yards	=	331.47 cm	=	3.31 m
3¾ yards	=	342.90 cm	=	3.43 m
3⅞ yards	=	354.32 cm	=	3.54 m
4 yards	=	365.76 cm	=	3.66 m
4⅛ yards	=	377.19 cm	=	3.77 m
4¼ yards	=	388.62 cm	=	3.89 m
4⅜ yards	=	400.05 cm	=	4.00 m
4½ yards	=	411.48 cm	=	4.11 m
4⅝ yards	=	422.91 cm	=	4.23 m
4¾ yards	=	434.34 cm	=	4.34 m
4⅞ yards	=	445.76 cm	=	4.46 m
5 yards	=	457.20 cm	=	4.57 m